BHĀSHĀBODHINĪ
A Sanskrit Reader

Sri Garib Das Oriental Series No. 353

BHĀSHĀBODHINĪ

A Sanskrit Reader

VOLUME - 3

Dr. MALAYA GANGOPADHYAY

SRI SATGURU PUBLICATIONS
A Division of :
INDIAN BOOKS CENTRE
DELHI (INDIA)

Published by :
SRI SATGURU PUBLICATIONS
Indological and Oriental Publishers
A Division of :
Indian Books Centre
14/6, Shakti Nagar,
Delhi-110 007 (INDIA)

First Edition : Delhi 2011

ISBN : 81-7030-934-4

Printed at : Sachin Printers, Delhi.

PREFACE

Long before Sir William Jones established a link between the European languages such as Greek, Latin, Celtic and Persian and Sanskrit in 1786, Fillipo Sassetti, an Italian merchant who lived in Goa from 1583 to 1588, found a definite relationship between Sanskrit and the European languages.

Subsequently the interest grew in Sanskrit and other Asian languages. The most notable Western Scholars of the nineteenth and twentieth centuries are Benfy, Max Muller, Roth, Whiney, Oldenberg, Weber, Burnell, Van Schroed, Bloomfield, Giffith Macdonell and Monier Williams, to name just a few.

However, Calmette's work on the *Ṛgveda* and the *Aitareya* Brahmana was the first notable contribution on Vedic literature. It may not be out of place to mention that much of the nineteenth century Western Scholars' inspiration in studying the ancient language and literature of distant lands was to prove the superiority of the Christian religion with the added hope of converting the 'heathens' to Christianity and India was no exception. There was another important aim as well, to perpetuate British colonialism and subjugation.

But there is no denying that their scholarship and writings had a tremendous impact on Indian intellectual development. Though the main source of Vedic studies was Sayanacharya's commentary, some traditional and modern Indian scholars did not entirely depend on his interpretations.

Swami Dyananda Sarasvati and his school, Sr Aurobinda Ghosh and Mahadeva Govinda Ranade are but a few of the modern thinkers who held different views, and they raised their voices against the prejudices shown by some European Scholars.

Swami Dayananda's opinion is that the Samhita portion of the Veda should be interpreted following Yaska's Nirukta, Pāṇini's Aṣṭādhyāyī and Patanjali's Mahābhāsya since etymology and grammar are indispensable for Vedic studies.

Sir Aurobinda considers that our modern mind is unable to fathom the depths of the ancient mind. Aurobinda and many other Indian scholars have disagreed with the predominant ritualistic interpretation of the Veda. In his view, the *Ṛṣis* guarded the sacred knowledge for the chosen few. It was restricted to those who are eager to know, while the elaborate sacrificial performance with respectful prayer and grandeur was prescribed for all. He emphasised the psychological import of the Vedic words and the symbolic character of the Vedic sacrifice. According to him, "the word for the vedic Ṛṣis is still a living thing, a thing of power, creative, formative. It is not yet a conventional symbol for an idea, but itself the parent and former of ideas... The letter lived on when the spirit was forgotten, the symbol, the body of the doctrine, remained, but the soul of knowledge had fled form its covering." (The Secret of the Vedas, pp. 51-57).

Theories of migration, Aryan invasion and a common stock of origin are well established. "It is now a commonplace of history that the Vedic Aryans and the Iranians descended form the same stock and exhibit great affinities and resemblance," writes Prof. Radhakrishnan (Indian Philosophy, Vol. 1, pp. 74). In Prof. Dasgupta's words : 'The hymns of the Rg-veda are neither the production of a single hand nor do they probably belong to any single age. They were composed probably at different periods indifferent sages, and it is not improbalde that some of them were composed before the Aryan people entered the plain of India... They reflect the civilization of the Aryan people at different periods of antiquity before and after they had come to India'. (A History of Indian Philosophy Vol. 1, pp. 14-15).

But it is strange that there is no hint anywhere in the literature about their original home. The theory that the Aryans were outsiders has not been satisfactorily settled. So far there is no archaeological proof of the Vedic ancestors original home, the Vedic people's migration or invasion. As for linguistic evidence, in the whole vast area of the Indian subcontinent there is no definite occurrence of a layer of non-Indo Aryan speech structure. The Indus valley culture covered a vast area form Sind, Baluchistan, Gujarat, Punjab, Haryana, Upper Rajasthan and Uttar Pradesh. It is difficult to identify who the Vedic people were and how they could have invaded and outnumbered the pre-Vedic people. How could they have imposed their own language to the extent of completely eliminating the local speech without leaving any trace of a single layer of its structure?

The lack of agreement between Scholars on this subject poses a challenge to all thinkers and is offered as a stimulating preamble.

CONTENTS

INTRODUCTION

Aspiration for a purpose is a genuine fact in human life. The notion of religion certainly can be considered as man's cognition of higher values for empirical life.

The term religion can be defined as man's attempt to understand the mysteries of life, the meaning of temporal existence. Not all people can be satisfied with a mere description of natural laws or a positive account of facts. The fundamental desire for knowing the unknown finds satisfaction in religion. It is a quest for the divine, that unknown factor which is considered to be the underlying principle of the universe.

Commonly the notion of religion is defined as an accepted value system which is perpetuated for a long period of time in a particular society. Form the functional point of view some characteristics can easily we categorised, including prayer to the unseen forces, for protection and social cohesion to bind the followers together, as well as the commonality in behaviour. It seems that the fundamental tenet of religion is to develop an attitude to life, creating a psychological base. Whether that psychological base results in widening the horizon of human understanding and elevating the mind, or conversely guarding, fencing around and limiting the boundary of mental expansion, depends on the teachings and their expression on the emphatic instructions and activities of each particular religion.

The Sanskrit equivalent for the term religion is dharma. Its meaning is wide, it includes the conducive behaviour, ethical moral values and obligatory social norms for the social man, as well as his spiritual enquiry : nīti, sadācāra and adhyātma jigñāsā are all suggested by this term.

In the words of a Western Scholar : the term includes not only religion but all the ethical, social and legal principles associated with religion and which together with it constitute the real meaning of life for the Hindu," (Louis Renou, Religion of Ancient India pp. 48).

The notion of religion is a complex one. There is a fine line between religion and spirituality in terms of semantic difference. From the functional point of view, the term religion has the connotation of involvement (svakāryamayatā), while spirituality indicates a detached beyondness. Its meaning includes the idea of a kind of limitless sublime feeling, which is not culturally bound. Often the experience is described as unspeakable joy, bliss, a feeling of oneness.

The great men of each epoch have indicated that while the religious approach is fundamentally based on the emotions, intellectual exercise cannot be discarded altogether. Maintaining ethical normal values is of the utmost importance and this in turn develops a certain attitude to life.

Looking at the world's great religions, we may come to the conclusion that the notion of religion includes both the higher realm of human thought and the pragmatic realm. The pragmatic realm covers the ethico-moral life with all its observances and following of dictates and dogmas, whereas the higher realm seeks the awakening of the mind and the dawning of spiritual wisdom.

Even though it is difficult to find an all-encompassing comprehensive definition that includes all its multi-dimensional facets, yet there are some fundamental tents of the notion as we understand :

developing a certain attitude,
looking form a particular perspective,
forming a kind of psychological base,
involvement in certain activities.

From the observable activities it is noticeable that the teachings, interpretation of the sacred texts (scriptures), ritualistic expression and the emphatic instructions and activities of each particular religion have a tremendous influence on its followers, even though the rituals and teachings, dictates and dogmas are but accessories to create a favourable atmosphere and arouse an individual's sentiment. Each religion has its cultural flavour and demands active group participation form its followers; but inspite of overt differences, at the core of all religions there is a deeper spiritual message.

Swami Vivekananda says :

'Mankind ought to be taught that religions are but the varied expressions of the Religion, which is oneness, so that each may choose the path that suits him best'. (Hinduism)

Etymologically, the term 'religion' in Latin and its equivalent 'dharma' in Sanskrit have a similar meaning : 'that which binds together'. The word dharma is derived form the root 'dhr' (धृ), meaning 'to uphold', bind'. According to Nirukta and later Dharmasastra, dharma means conducive rules and regulations that sustains the world and human society. The qualities such as non-violence (ahimsā), non-stealing (āsteya), non-anger (akrodha), forgiveness (kshmā), compassion (daya), self-control (samjama), friendliness (sahrdayata), and lawful progeny, maintaining caste duties and truth-justice (sataya) etc. are considered to be components of dharma by the Smrti, Darshana and the

Mahābhābhārata. In Bhaktivāda dharma is intuitive contemplation .These authoritative works highlight the social significance of religion. But merely following the conducive rules and regulations does not raise the mind to the higher state. Those with an enquiring mind will test themselves by analysing their own mental activity. Traditionally, whatever we inherit we follow, but the enquiring mind may not be satisfied with mechanical activities. So to accommodate individual temperaments several paths are suggested in Hinduism.

Only when it encompasses the psychic, philosophical and social realms does the notion of religion become wholesome. In Swami Vivekananda's words : 'Religion speaks of ....the moral, ethical and spiritual relations between soul and soul, between individual sprit and the father of all spirits.'

We may sum up that religion is a sublime human aspiration, however crude, primitive or sophisticated it may be, it refers to the higher realm of human thought.

SECTION 1

THE SACRED TEXTS

The Veda is the most ancient scripture of the Indian subcontinent, and is regarded as the divine book of eternal knowledge by the Hindus. It is the main source of Brahmanical thoughts (philosophy).

The Samhitā portion is divided into four collections. They are the Rk, Yaju, Sāma and Atharvan. These are the four Vedas. Ṛgveda contains 10522 verses, Yajurveda 1984, Sāmaveda 1875 and Atharvaveda 5977 totalling 20358 in numbers.

The Rk-Samhitā is the earliest. The hymns (Rc) are for invoking deities, and expressing innumerable ideas which can be interpreted in terms of various dimensions. Once again we are using Swami Vivekananda's words : the Veda is the 'accumulated treasury of spiritual laws....that govern the world'.

There were five sākhās of the Ṛgveda - the Sākala, the Bāskala, the Asvalāyana, the Sānkhāyana and the Māndukya. Only the recension of Sākala is extant.

Patanjali's Mahabhasya speaks of 101 branches (śākhā) of the Yajurveda, of which only a few are extant: Kānva, Mādhyadini, Taittiriya, Maitreyani, Kāṭhaka and Kapisthala.

The word Yajus means sacrifice. The Taittiriya Samhitā and the Vājasanya Samhitā are known as Kṛṣṇa (black) and Sukla (white) Yajurveda respectively, they contain hymns

(Ṛc) form the Ṛgveda and prose passages explaining the rules for the performance of rituals.

The four main deities associated with each are : the Sun with Ṛk, Fire with Yaju, Air with Sama and the Moon with Atharvan. They rule over the elements of nature, the natural process and human physical-mental activities. It is regarded that the Ṛṣis received them by means of divine revelation.

Prof. Radhakrishnan writes : 'The Rgveda Samhita or collection contains of 1,017 hymns or Suktas... It is divided into eight aṣṭakas, each having eight adhyāyas or chapters, which are further sub-divided into vargas or groups. It is some times divided into ten mandalas or circles. The latter is the more popular division.' (Indian Philosophy Vol. 1 p. 67).

The Ṛgveda and Yajurveda spak of the origin of Ṛc, sāma, Chandas and Yaju that all emanated from the Sarvahuta *yajña* (sacrifice). In the Puruṣa sutra of the Ṛgveda (10/90) we find the expressions :

tasmād yajñāt sarvahuta Ṛc sāmani jajñira/
chandansi jajñire tasmād yajustasmād jāyata//

Form the Sarvahuta yajña all Ṛk and Sāma hymns were evolved, the Vedic meters and Yaju mantras were exhibited.

In the first mandala 191 hymns are arranged addressing different gods. Agni is the main deity in the Rgveda. The very first sukta is :

agnim iṛe purohitam/
yajñyasya devam ṛtvijam/
hotāram ratnadhatamam//

'I praise Agni, domestic priest, God, minister of sacrifice, Herald, Most prodigal of wealth.' (Tr. Prof.

Macdonell, History of Sanskrit literature.) Indra, Mitra, Varuna, Marut, Surya, Asvin, Matarisvan, Soma and Parjanya are the main male Vedic deities. The female deities include Usas, Aditi, Sindhu, Sarasvati, Vāk and Araṇyāni. The river Sarasvati was the heart, both physical and spiritual, of Vedic civilization.

Most Vedic gods were classified by Prof. Dasgupta 'as terrestrial atmospheric and celestial'. (History of Indian Philosophy Vol. 1, pp. 17). In Prof. Radhakrishnan's words: 'Naturalism and anthropomorphim seem to be first stage of the vedic religion'. (Indian Philosophy Vol. 1, pp. 74). Some scholars consider that the gods of the hymns are symbols of the psychological function : the Sun God Surya 'signifies intelligence, Agni-will, and Soma-feeling'. This point of view is different from that of modern European Scholoars and their Indian followers and does not tally with tradition either. Modern scholoars are of the opinion that the stories of conflict among the deva and asura, the naga etc. are the recorded history of the Aryans and other settlers in the land. Many of the demons, the foes of Indra are the tribal Gods or heros. One of them was the 'deified hero' (kṛṣṇa?) on the banks of Amsumati (Jamunā) river.

Yajña is a kind of complicated ritualistic performance of elaborate fire oblation with chanting appropriate mantras. The purpose of yajña is the accomplishment of material desires (Sankalpa Siddhi). The hymns (mantras) are selected according to the presiding deity. When duly performed, exactly and flawlessly, it is destined to produce its desired effect : the yajña has 'mystical potency'.

Gradually the scrificial rite came to be regarded as the only duty or action (karma). Eventually the performance dominated, for karma has to be performed. One class of people was entrusted to do the elaborate (action) ceremony, which is no longer the simple action of lighting the Gārhapatya agni, the family fire worship. Several priests trained in this special activity, do the job on behalf of the one, for whom the sacrifice was arranged, the yajamāna,–who is not involved in the actual performance. His role is of the organiser, supplier and passive recipient of the boon. Though the deities are still to be invoked, the formal complicated actions replaced the devotion and wonder of the Vedic poetic mind.

The Sāmaveda contains hymns nearly all form the Ṛgveda, which are chanted by the Udgātri priest at all time of yajña. Besides the hymns for chanting, mention is made of Upāsanā (worship and contemplation). It has two parts Purva-ārcika and Uttara-ārcika. The Purra–arcika has two manuals. The Gramageya–gama and Aranyageyagana one for the common congregation and the other for the forest recluse. Of the original one thousand branches of the Sāmaveda only three survived : Kauthumā in Gujarāt, Rānāyaniya in Maharastry and Jaiminiya in Karnātaka. The Sāmaveda is of great importance to the priests :

sāmavedo brahmanānām prasuti/

It is not very different form the Ṛgveda samhitā. At the time of yajña, suitable and appropriate Ṛc containing verse and sukta were to be recited or sung. These tuned verses or hymns are known as Sāman and the arranged Samans form the Ṛk-samhitā is the Sāma-samhita or Sāmaveda.

The Atharvaveda covers many topics, including hymns to Prithivi, marriage, many names of medicine and formulae for healing diseases, outlines of popular beliefs and religious rites, the importance of Japa, as well as prayers for good health, wealth, longivity and protection. The Atharva veda has 20 kāṇḍa (divisions) covering various subjects : the glorification of creation, the elements of nature, homage to several gods, the river Sarasvati, yajña, the earth, the atmosphere, human activities and so on. It contains prayers for protection from evil, for good food and good harvest, nourishment and strength. There are secular sides on healing, medicine and rules of conduct. It records the early history of the scientific enquiry of the Aryan people in the fields of mathematics, medicine, architecture, geometry, alchemy etc.

In Prof. Radhakrishnan's words : 'magic and mysticism soon become confused'. (*ibid.*, pp. 121). In this text we find hymns of Kāla (time), Kāma (love) and Skambha (support), who is identified with Prajāpati, Purusa and Brahman. In the Rgveda the word Śiva means auspicious while in the Atharvaveda, Rudra Śiva is the Lord Pasupati. Female deities become prominent, cow is recognised as sacred, the Brahamaloka and Naraka (heaven and hell) are mentioned.

This text was originally called Atharvāñgirash meaning Atharvan and Angiras (two names). Later it became incorporated in to the category of the Vedas. The Atharva-veda states that Ṛc and Yaju have originated in time :

kālād ṛc sambhavan yaju kālād jāta/

As yajña is for the prosperity of the community, man has to make an effort if he wishes to obtain the desired end. 'Vedic knowledge is mastered though toil and holy fervour': sramena tapasā sṛsta. Glorification of the directions, the atmosphere, yogic practice and brahmacarya etc. are found in many verses side by side with magical charms. The Atharva veda is a combination of both.

There we find some beautiful hymns :

mātā bhumi putra aham prthibyah/
parjanyah pitā sa o nah pipartu//

The Earth is my mother, I am the son of Earth, the cloud is my father, may it nourishes us.

tasyai hiranyavakshase pṛthibya akaranam/

Of mother Earth with golden breast I render my adoration.

Prof. Radhakrishnan thinks 'the Atharva veda is an amalgam of Aryan and non-Aryan ideas. (pp. 120). He also says 'the Atharva veda helped to prepare the way for the scientific development in India. (pp. 123)

Two of nine branches of the Atharvaveda are extant : Saunaka and Pippalāda. (ii)

Many profound and significant concepts appear in the Ṛgveda, including the idea of Ṛta and Tadekam, the idea of creation and the use of the neuter term Sat. The Ṛṣis are mantradraṣṭā *i.e.* 'seers' of the mantras (hymns). They cognised that there is an order that maintains the world and beyond, and thus it is necessary to follow the path of Ṛta.

Ṛtasya panthānam pasya/(Atharvaveda)

Ṛta means the order, law that maintains the physical and the moral world. It is the divine truth form which arises the perception of unity and harmony.

Ekam sat viprā bahudhā vadanti/

The One is addressed by different names by the wise sages. The Ṛsis declare that water is the primal matter and Visvakarman is the creator of the universe, the first born the world egg floating on this water is the primordial germ of life.

Purusa eva idam sarvam yad bhutam yacca bhavyam/

(Ṛgveda 10/90) Purusa is the source and ground of all, pervading all existence, past present and future. The Devisūkta was composed by Ṛsi Vāc, the daughter of Abhrna Ṛsi.

The Ṛgveda contains the Sāvitri mantra :

tat saviturvarenyam bhargo devasya dhimahi/
dhiyo yo nah prachodayāt// (Ṛgveda iii. 62.10)

'The adorable glory of Sāvitri, Deva, we contemplate; may he arouse our intellect'.

Earth Heaven and Eather (atmosphere) : Bhur, Bhuvah Sva - are added in the Yajurveda.

The Seven Vedic Poetic Metres (Chandas) : Gāyatri, Ushnik, Anushtup, Bṛhatti, Pankti, Tṛshtup and Jagati, are linked with specific colours and notes :

sita sāranga piśanga kṛṣṇa nila lohita varṇā/
ṣaṛajaṛṣabha gāṅdhāra madhyamā paṅcama
dhaivatam niṣāda svarāh//

The colours are white, variegated, tawny, black, blue and red; the seven notes of the Indian musical scale : sa, re, gā, mā, pā, dhā and ni. It is believed that the second and fifth sounds are produced by the cow and cuckoo respectively.

In the Yajurveda some mantras have extra laudatory words or phrases, called Nivid, Ṛk mantras with added Nivid are known as yajus.

In this text we find the assertion that by performing yajña man will attain wealth' projeny, long life, strength and power; in other words, earthly well being, By performing yajña man becomes free form diseases.

Although the ritualistic performance is emphasised, there other ideas are also expressed in various ślokas :

Traymbakam yajāmahe sugandhim puṣṭivardhnam/
urvārukamiva vandhanātmaṛtyormushiya māmṛtam/

(*Chapter 3, sloka 60*)

To Trayambaka our offerings :

To the fragrance-bearer, the increaser of nourishment : May he release me, like the cucumber form the stem, form mortal life, not from immortality. (Tr. by Abinash Chandra Bose).

na tasya pratimā asti (*Chapter 32, sloka 1*)

There is no image of Him.

mitrasyaham cakṣhusā sarvāni bhutāni samikṣhe/
mitrasya cakshusā samikṣhāmahe//

(*Chapter 33, sloka 18*)

'The eleventh chapter speaks of intellectual cultivation. In chapter thirtyone, verse 16 mentions mental contemplation, and the famous utterance of Upanisad :' vedahametam... nānya panthā vidyate ayanāya', is found in verse No. 18. The verse 19 says that the Yogis realise His (God's) true nature; the whole existing world stands on Him, the ground of all. In chapter thirtythree, verse three contains the well know form of the Gayatri mantra. Verse 20 of chapter thirtyseven is the famous utterance :

pitā no asi pitā no bodhi namaste astu/
mā mā hinsih //

'Tumi āmāder pitā, tomay pitā bole yena jāni tomay nato hoye yeno māni, tumi koronā koronā ros' (Tagore's translation in Bangali).

You are our father, we know, we bow to you (thee), do not show your (thy) wrath. The last verse of chapter forty is:

hiranmayena pātrena satyasya nihitam mukham/
'The face of truth is covered with a golden lid......'

(Tr.Abinash c. Bose)

Sāyanacarya's interpretation is widely accepted. He placed more emphasis on the Abhyudaya-gaining merits by the performance of rituals.

Brāhmana

The 'Brāhmana' texts are the further development of the Samhitā. Written in prose, they explain the significance of the rituals. The next development is the 'Aranyaka', a system for the forest dwellers, which covers the symbolic presentation of rituals, together with suggested meditation. It shows that the outward worship has progressed towards a more internal, inward looking process, gradually leading to the philosophic speculation of the Upaniṣad.

The dimensions of Vedic society into four broad classes are mentioned in the Purusa-sūkta (Ṛgveda 10. 136. 3), and the Atharvaveda says man becomes powerful by observing dharma and gaining caturvarga (the four desired ends). The ideas of Varṇa, Varga and Āśrama are very significant. The word Varṇa in this context should be understood as follows:

The description of the characteristics or traits of the four classes :

The learned, intellectually advanced Brahmins, the protectors or rulers Ksatriyas, those who are earning wealth, growing food the Vaisyas, and those who are tilling in the soil, giving in service to society the Sudras. Although it began as a kind of occupational social groupings, later the system became rigid and hereditary.

'The daily pursuits of man' - Kṣhatra, Sravas, Iṣṭa and Artha *i.e.*, maintaining order, the pursuit of fame, the pursuit of desired objects and work for living - are mentioned in the Ṛgveda. These activities are crystalised as the four fold aims of human life, indicating the idea of Caturvarga : dharma, artha, kāma, mokṣha. While the upholders of maintaining rules and order are the Kṣhatriyas, the Sravas are the Ṛṣis, the learned. They are the recipients of the mantra, they search for truth and are detached worldly concerns-mokṣhakāmī. Those who increase the social wealth through trade and commerce is the class of vaisya and the workingmen śudra, the custodians of all sorts of required work in society.

The Ṛgveda Speaks of Agriculture : Ploughing, the plough, the furrow and the cow are all personified. The Atharvaveda speaks about Āśramadharma - (*i*) Brahmacaryā (studentship) : a life of discipline, training and learning, (*ii*) Gārhapatya : the householder life. The family is considered to be the basis of society and marriage is a sacrament; (*iii*) Pravrajyā : the life of the spiritual wanderer. The word āśrama is the extension of the word śrama, meaning 'to toil'. The second word is a conbination of gṛha and āptyā, meaning home and family. The other one meaning 'to roam about'.

Traditionally there are two main divisions in the Vedas: the Karma-kānda and the Jñāna-kānda. Karma is the path of action, aimed at achieving earthly wellbeing. Jñāna is the path of spiritual knowledge. The necessary requirements for both are discipline, effort, knowledge, intelligence and strength. Intelligence (dhi) kindles spiritual fire (tapas)-higher enquiry and attention to the innerself produces niśreyasa. Karma accepts social activities, yielding abhyudaya, but karma is never detached form the preception of the innerworld.

These are some of the Ṛṣis who composed the hymns of the Ṛgveda

Aghamarsana, Agastya, Ayasya, Apratirtha, Dirghatamas, Gṛtsamada, Gotama, Gargā, Bhaumā, Bhikshu, Bharadvāja, Medhātithi, Damana, Madhuchandas, Manu, Hiranyagarbha, Nemā, Nabhak, Nārāyaṇa, Prajāpati, Priyamedha, Parucchepa, Śiśu, Savya, Śatyasrava, Sindhudvipa, Syavasva, Sunahotra, Samkusuka, Syumarasmi, Samvanana, Syavasva, Tirasci, Triśoka, Vāmadeva, Vaśiṣṭha, Viśwāmitra, Vṛhaspati etc.

Some Ṛṣikā (Female Composers)

Apālā Ātreyi, Ghosā, Indrani, Kākshivati, Saci-Paulomi, Vāk, Yami.

The hymns of the Ṛgveda are the source of the later development of the iconic approach in Hinduism : the Devisūkta, Puruṣa sūkta, Hiranyagarva (the Golden egg) and Viśvakarman (creator of all) are but a few examples.

The Veda is known as Śruti, maning 'heard'. It implies that the knowledge is intuitive experience, intuitive feeling that was expressed in words. So Vāk i.e., speech is considered as the mother of the Vedas - 'Vedamātā Gāyatri', 'Vedānām mātā'. Gāyatri is a name of a Vedicmetre. The word Veda is derived form the root vid 'to know'.

Brāhmana texts are attached to each collection of Veda. Composed in prose, most of them deal with the rituals and explaining their significance. Those which give directions are known as Vidhi, and those which give explanations, are known as Arthavād including stories, philosophical speculations and exegetical explanations. Many are now lost, which is understood from quotations found in the extant texts. The Satapatha Brāhmana is a very important one : the names of many countries mentioned appear to indicate that during that time Eastern India was the leading authority. The Yājñavalkya was form Videha (Tirhut), although the centre of brāhamanical culture was still the land of the Kuru-Pāñcāla. Janamejaya was the king of the Kurus, the great teacher Āruni was a native of Pāñcāla. During that time the court of king Jaṅaka at Mithilā was prominent; there several distinguished teachers of the Western region had accepted the leadership of the Eastern teachers. In the Satapatha the Gautama family of Kapilavastu is mentioned, and the words Arhat, Śramana etc. are found. The stories of Pururavā-Urvasi, Bharata-Śakuntalā appear in full form. It gives details on how to construct the fire alter, the name of a teacher who is traditionally known as the founder of Sāmkhya system (Āsuri). This Brāhmana text is a store house of important information. It belongs to White Yajurveda. There are two recensions of the Mādhyadina and the Kānva schools.

There are three schools of Black Yajurveda the Kaṭha, the Maitrayani, and the Taittiriya have Brāhmana texts.

The Aitareya, the Sānkhayana and the Kausitaki Brāhmans are attached to the Ṛgveda. The Pancavimsa (Tānḍya/Praudha), the Saḍvimsa, the Adbhuta, the Chāndogya, the Sāmavidhāna, the Devatādhyaya, the Vansa Brahmana texts belongs to Sāmaveda. The Tānḍya gives details of Soma yajña, several stories, the details of rituals performed on the Sarasvatī and Dṛsadvatī rivers. It is very interesting to know that the Vrātya-sṭama was meant for the men to enter in Brāhmanical order.

Āraṇyaka

The later portions of the Brāhmana literature developed into the Āraṇyaka stage where the interest is shifted form the sacrificial performance to inward enquiry in the solitude of nature. Āraṇayaka refers to 'forest text', meant for people who have retired to forest dwellings *i.e.*, living in Āśrama.

Further continuation in the same line gave rise to the Upaniṣadic character of the Vedic literature. The Upaniṣad stage does not represent the ritual performance or karma (the 'practical side'). Its sole enquiry is of Ātman-Brahman. Its aspiration is for knowledge, Jñāna, and in particular ātmajiñāsā *i.e.*, self enquiry, to know the real nature of the self. With the Upaniṣad we have arrived at the concluding stage of the Vedic literature. The word Upaniṣad implies a secret or confidential discussion; the literal meaning is 'sitting down close by'.

From the hymns and prayers, homage and invocation to Purusa, Viśvadeva, Prajāpati, Varuṇa, Ṛta other Divinities developed the concept of Brahman/Ātman the vital breath, which was gradually abstracted into the impersonal world-essence, the unknown Cosmic divinity pervading everything, the entire creation including human activity like rituals and sacrifice, concluded in the equation of Brahman, the cosmic principle, and Ātman, the physical principle of individual.

Diagramatic Summary, Vedic literature
(The word Veda's in derived from the root Vid 'to know')

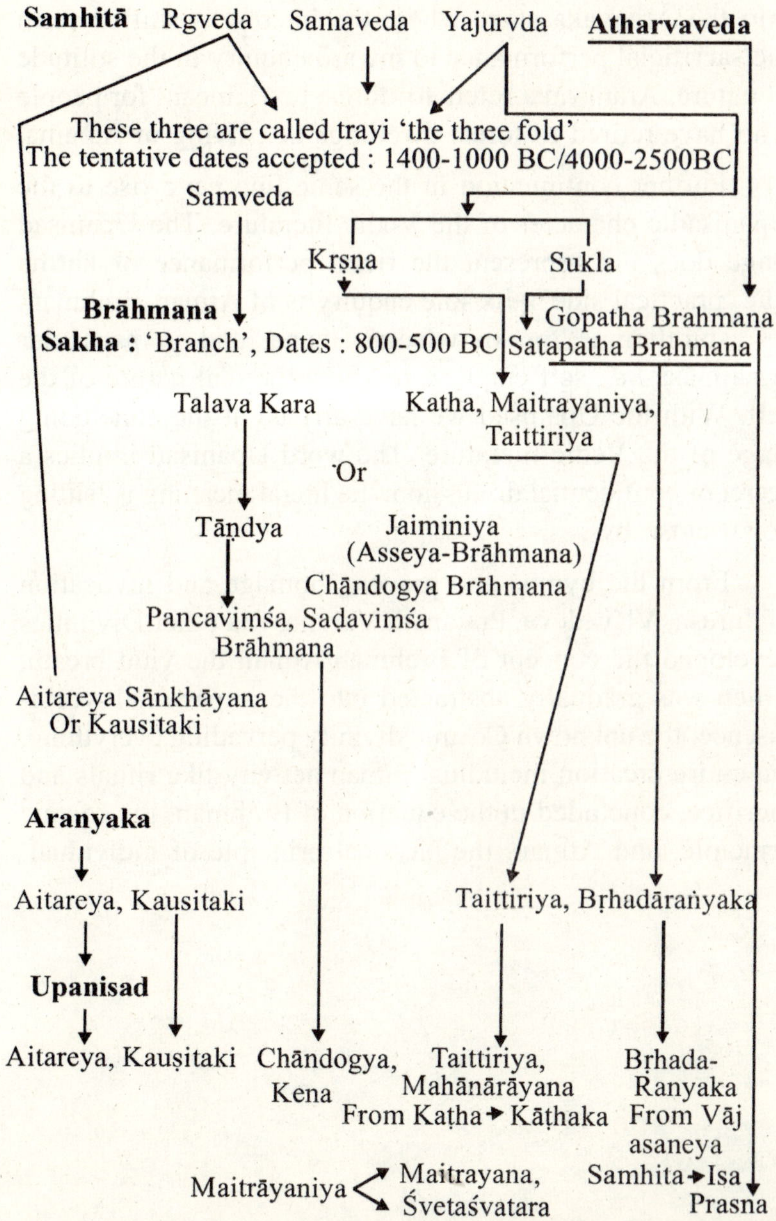

Praśna, Mundaka and Māndukya Upanisads belong to Atharvaveda and they belong to the Pippalāda, Māndukya, Saunaka Sakhas respectively.

There were 108 Upanisad in number. Not all are extant. Śamkara Ācharya has commented upon 11(10) of them in 9th Century. There is a controversy regarding Śvetaśvatara. Śamkara did not comment on Kausitaki.

Besides Śamkara, Ramānujācarya in the 12th Century, Madhvācarya in the 13th Century and Valadeva in the 18th Century wrote commentaries on the 10 Upanisads. Apart form Śamkarācarya's commentary the others are based on the devotional attitude.

In the earlier Upaniṣads the attitude was not necessarily devotional; it was positively enquiring, questioning, striving to grasp the truth. The word 'bhakti' is first categorically mentioned in Śvetasvatara Upaniṣad and the concept of devotion probably flourished form that time onward.

Brahman or Akṣhara or Ātma of Bhūmā is the essence of the Universe. It is Unknown, blessed is he whoever received the grace, through earnest effort, knowledge dawns upon him; sharpening the intelligence, acquiring knowledge and with the deepest feeling of heart Truth may be revealed.

The animate inanimate everything is pervaded by the same power or energy or essence that is Brahman : Prajñā.

The Aitareya Upaniṣad says :

sarvam tat prajñānetram prajñāne, pratiṣṭhitam prajñānetre lokah prāṇa pratisṭhā prajñānam brahma/ (3.1.3)

According to Sankarācarya eighteen of the extant 108 Upanisads are authentic. He wrote commentaries on the Isa,

Kena, Kaṭha, Praśna, Muṇḍaka, Māṇḍukya, Taittiriya, Aitareya, Chāndogya and Bṛhdāranyaka Upanisads and used quotations from the other six in his commentary on the Brahmasūtra. Regarding the Śvetaśvatara Upaniṣad scholars have a different opinion. They are not in agreement that there is any commentary written by Śankarācārya.

Some Information Regarding Translation

"Dārā Shiko, the eldest son of the Emperor Shah Jahan, heard of the Upanisads during his stay in Kashmir in 1640. He invited several Pandits form Benares to come to Delhi, where they took the work of translating then into Persian. In 1775 Anquetil Duperron, the discoverer of the Zend-Avesta, received a manuscript of it presented to him by his friend Le Gentil, a French resident in Faizabad at the court of Shuja-Uddaulah. Anquetil translated it into Latin and it was published in 1801-1802. This translation though largely unintelligible, was read by Schopenhauer with great enthusiasm. It had, as Schopenhaur himself admits, a profound influence on his philosophy....Through Schopenhauer, the study of the Upaniṣads attracted much attention in Germany and with the growth of a general interest in the study of Sanskrit, the works found their way into other parts of Europe as well."

The study of the Upaniṣads however gained great inpetus form the earnest attempts of Ram Mohan Roy who not only translated them into Bengali, Hindi and English and published them at his own expense, but also founded the Brahma Samaj in Bengal, the main religious doctrine of which were derived form the Upaniṣads." (S. Dasgupta, A History of Indian Philosophy Vol. 1 pp. 39-40).

In 1799 Sir William Jones translated Isa Upanisad. Later Prof. Max Muller translated most of them.

The names of the Upanisads and where they belong to:

Aitareya	Ṛgveda Aitareya Āraṇyaka
Kauṣitaki	Ṛgveda Śāṅkhāyana Āraṇyaka
Kena	Sāmaveda Jaiminiya Brāhmana
Chāndogya	Sāmaveda Chāndogya Brāhmana
Taittiriya	Kṛṣṇa Yajurveda Taittiriya Āraṇyaka
Bṛhadāraṇyaka	Sukla Yajurveda Satapath Brāhmana
Isa	Sukla Yajurveda Vājasaneya Samhitā
Kaṭha	Kṛṣṇa Yajurveda Taittiriya Brāhmana
Śvetaśvatara	Traditionally, Kṛṣṇa Yajurveda
Muṇḍaka	Traditionally, Atharvaveda Śaunaka sākhā
Prasna	Atharvaveda Paippalāda sākhā
Māṇdukya	Atharvaveda Māṇḍukya Sākha

Some of the Great Saying (Mahāvākya)

Prajñānam brahma *Aitareya Upanisad* (3.1.3)

etat evahi akṣhram brahma
Kaṭha Upaniṣad (1.2 valli, 16)

tat tvam asi chāndagya upanisad (6.8.7)

sarvam khalu idam brahma
Kaṭha Upaniṣad (3.14.1)

ānando brahmati vyajanāt
Taittiriya Upanisad (3.6.1)

omiti brahma *Taittiriya Upanisad* (i.8.1)

raso vai sah *Taittiriya Upanisad* (2.7.2)

sa akāmayata bahu syām

Taittiriya Upanisad (2.6.3)

**śraddheyā deyam/ asraddheyā adeyam/
śriyā deyam/hṛiyā deyam/bhiyā deyam/
samvidā deyam/**

Taittiriya Upanisad (1.12.3)15

satyam vada/ dharmam cara/ sādhyāyam mā pramādah/

Taittiriya Upanisad (1.11.1)

**mātṛ deva bhava/ pitṛ deva bhava/
ācarya deva bhava/ atithi deva bhava/
yani anavadyāni karmani/ tāni sevitavyāni/
no itarāni/**

Taittiriya Upanisad (1.11.2)

**yenāham nāmṛta syām kim aham tena kurjām/
(Maitrayi said)**

Bṛhadāraṇyaka Upaniṣad (2.4.3)

**asato mā sadgamaya tamso mā jyotirgamaya
mṛtyor māmṛtam gamaya/**

Bṛhadāraṇyaka Upaniṣad (1.4.28)

**īśā vāsyamidam sarvam yatkinca jagatyām jagat/
tena tyāktena bhunjithā mā gṛdha kasyasid dhanam//**

Iśa Upaniṣad (1)

ananda rupam amṛtam yadvibhāti//

Muṇḍaka Upaniṣad (2.2.8)

**satyam eva jayāte nānṛtam satyena panthā
vitato devayām/**

Muṇḍaka Upaniṣad (3.1.6)

**nāyamātmā pravacanena labhya na medhayā na
bahunhā śrutena/**

yamevaisa vṛnute tena labhyastasyaiṣa ātmā
vivṛnute tanum svām//

Muṇḍaka Upaniṣad (3.2.3)

nāyamātma balahīnema labhya naca pramādāt
tapaso vāpyālingāt/

Muṇḍaka Upaniṣad (3.2.4)

śāntam śivam advaitam caturtham manyante/
sa ātmā/sa vijñeyah//

Maṇḍukya Upaniṣad (7)

anorāniām mahato mahiyānātmasya jantornihito
guhāyam/

Kaṭha Upanisad (1.2.20)
also in *Svetasvatara Upaniṣad* (3.20)

uttisṭhata jāgrata prāpya varāṇ nibodhata/
kṣhurasya dhārā niśitā durātyayā/
durgam pathstāt kavayo vadanti//

Kaṭha Upanisad (1.3.14)

na tatra suryo bhāti na candra tārakam nemā
vidyuta bhānti kutoyam agnih/
tameva bhāntamanubhāti sarvam tasya bhāsā
sarvamidam vibhāti//

Kaṭha Upanisad (2.2.15)

vedahametam pursṣam mahantam adityavarṇam
tamasah parstāt/
tameva viditvaeti mṛtyumeti nānyah panthā
vidyate ayanāya//

Śvetaśvatara Upaniṣad (3.8)

śṛnvantu viśve amṛtasya putrā ā ye dhāmāni
divyāni tasthuh//

Śvetaśvatara Upaniṣad (2.5)

yo devo agno yo apsu yo viśvam bhuvanam āviveśa/
ya oṣadhīṣu yo vanaspatiṣu tasmai devāyā namo namah//

Śvetaśvatara Upaniṣad (2.17)

The above mentioned quotations give a fair idea that the aspiration, attitude and the subject matter found in the ending part of the Vedic literature are characteristically distinct form the preceding portions. The upaniṣads record the seers' thoughts, ideas, experiences, insights and realisations. They do not constitute any philosophical system, neither are they logically consistent in nature. Some are recorded in prose form while some are in poetry and some are narrated as dialogue. In some texts prose and poetry are combined. The method of exposition differs : there are stories, narrations of events, legends, instructions, counsel, advice and sermons.

The word 'upaniṣad' indicates that the teaching is meant for earnest enquirers who are self disciplined.

The Kena starts with questions then the teacher gives an exposition, explaining the great saying :

ātmānā vindate viryam/
vidyayā vindate amṛtam// (2.4)

'He who realises the existence of Brahman behind every activity of his being... he alone gains immortality. Through knowledge of Brahman comes power. Through knowledge of Brahman comes victory over death.'

(Tr.Swami Prabhabananda and Frederic Manchester)

Who is the teacher and who is the pupil? - there is no name.

The Kaṭha Gives a Senario : Ṛṣi Vājaśravasa performs he viśvajit sacrifice. While the gifts (offering cows to the riests) are being given away, the child Naciketā asks his ather (Vājaśravasa) to whom he will be offered? And his ather says 'I offer you to Death'. The legend starts there; Naciketā, the young lad visits the abode of Yama the king of Death. Naciketā asks question, resists temptation and ıltimately attains the true knowledge of life and death.

In the Praśna Upaniṣad the teacher Pippalāda answers questions asked by his six disciples on the six main points of Vedānta. In Muṇḍaka Ṛṣi Angiras answers the questions out by Ṛṣi Śaunaka. The Taittiriya is divided in three parts: Śikṣhāvallī, Brahmānḍavallī and Bhṛguvallī. It is recorded n a form of dialogue between son and father, Bhṛgu the son and father Varuṇa.

The Iśa is the last chapter of the Vājasaneyi Samhitā of he Sukla Yajurveda. It is also known as the Samhitopaniṣad, contains the fundamentals of the Vedānta philosophy.

The Bṛhadāranyaka contains the last 14th part of the Śatapatha Brāhamana, starting with an allegorical explanation of the horse sacrifice. It contains four philosophical discourses in dialogue form, including dispute among the scholars and a dialogue with king Janaka.

The main speaker is Yājñavalkya, who discusses with his second wife, Brahmavādinī Maitreyī, as well as answering questions raised by Gārgi.

The Chāndogya is composed of the 8 chapters of the Chāndogya Brāhamana of the Tāṇḍya branch of the Sāmaveda. It deals with various topics; it contains several tories, and many peoples' names are mentioned there : Jsanticakrāyana, Janaśruti pautrāyana, Raikka, Kakshasena,

Abhipratari, Satyakāma jāvāla, Gautama, Upakosalakamalāyana, Gosruti, Śvetaketu, Pravāhana, Jival, Aruṇi Asvapati, Uddalaka, Prāciśāta, Pulusa, Ballavi, Indradyumna, Śarkarāksha, Asvatarāsva, Buril, Nārada, Santkumāra, Prajāpati, Índra, Virocana etc. Some are pupils, some are teachers.

Ṛṣi Śvetāśvatara is the author of the Śvetaśvatara Upaniṣad, which is recorded in poetry.

Some of the names of the great teachers of the Upanisads:

Mahidāsa Aitareya, Satyakāma Jābāla, Uddālaka, Śvetaketu Bālāki, Ajātaśatru, Varuṇa, Yājñavalkya, Pratardana Gargāyana, as well as the Ṛṣikā Maitreyī and Gārgi.

We conclude this discussion with a quotation form Prof. Macdonell :

"Brahma (neuter) in the Ṛgveda signified nothing more than 'prayer' or 'devotion'. But even in the oldest Brāhmanas it has come to have the sense of 'Universal holiness', as manifested in prayer, priest and sacrifice. In the Upaniṣads it is the holy principle which animates nature. Having a long subsequent history this word is a very epitome of the evolution of religious thought in India. These two conceptions Ātman and Brāhman, are commonly treated as synonymous in the Upaniṣads. But strictly speaking, Brāhmana the older term, represents the cosmical principle which pervades the universe, Ātman the physical principle manifested in man; and the letter, as the known, is used to explain the former as unknown." (History of the Sanskrit Literature, pp. 185).

(vide Bṛhadāranyaka, 111.V111.8.ii ; Kaṭha, 1V.9, V1.9. 12; Chāndogya, V1.8-16).

The religion of the Veda Brahmana do not propagate harm, injury or killing. The Upanisadic enquiry centres around Brhaman-Ātman. The philosophical ideas accommodates various speculations of differing opinions.

Sutra Texts

The Vedic hymns were metrical, the Yajurveda and Brahmana literature are expressed in prose, down through the Āranyaka-Upanisad a combination of prose and poetry are found. Thereafter developed a very concise form of expression, which is known as Śutra(aphorism), approximately in 500-200 B.C.

Both Karmakāṇḍa and Jñānakāṇḍa are continued in this form. There are several Śutra texts attached to the various branches of the four Vedas. These texts are of three types (categories) which are not considered as revealed : Śrauta, Gṛhya and Dharma.

(*i*) **Śrauta :** It is concerning with the rituals, regarding Yajña rules and sacrificial directions.

The well known Śrauta Sūtras are :

Ṛgveda : Śānkhāyana, Aśvalāyana.

Yajurveda : Sukla : Kātyāyana; Kṛṣṇa : Apastamba, Hiranyakeśin, Baudhāyana and Mānavas.

Sāmaveda : Lātyāyana, Maśaka's Kalpa or Ārṣeya Kalpa, Drāhyāyana.

Atharvaveda : Vaitāna Sūtra : 'Relating to the sacrificial fires'. It is not recorded in anybody's or many group's name. The whole body of the Śrauta sūtra is also known as Kalpa sūtra. The Śrauta rites are fourteen in number and they are performed on behalf of the Yajamāna by the priests. The beginning ceremony is agniādhāna, 'the setting up of the sacred fire', lit up by the Yajamāna and his wife, which should be maintained by giving havis (oblation) twice daily. This is known as Agnihotra. The other two are darśapūrṇamāsa and caturmāsyā. The new and full moon yajña and offering giving at the beginning of three seasons respectively. Besides these there are Agniṣtoma, *i.e.*, Somayajña of various kinds and various ceremonies for attainment of something desired by the Yajamāna.

(*ii*) **Gṛhya :** It is concerning with the samskāras-domestic rites required to be performed form the birth to death, the whole span of life.

The domestic rituals are not mentioned in the Brāhmana portion. Some of the Gṛhya Sūtras are continuation of the Śrauta Sūtra, some are independently composed.

Belonging to the Ṛgveda Sākhā are Śānkhāyana, Sambavya, Aśvalāyana.

Belonging to the Sāmaveda Sākhā are Gobhila and Khadira.

Belonging to the Sukla Yajurveda Sākhā are Pāraskara or Vājasaneya.

Belonging to the Kṛṣṇa Yajurveda Sākhā are Āpastambha, Hiranyakesin.

Mānava (the worship of Vināyakas is mentioned in this text for the first time), Bodhāyana, Kāṭhak, Vaikhānasa, Bharadvāja.

Belonging to the Atharvaveda are Kausika Sūtra. It mentions numerous rites of domestic life, forty samaskāras (sacraments), student life, inauguration of kings, benediction, purification, building and entering into a new house, funeral, utsarga (offering monuments) etc.

(*iii*) **Dharma :** It is based on tradition and known as Smṛti concerning with the social legal rules of conduct, customs of every day life (sāmayācārika or sadācarā), Law book and polity.

The well known Dharma Sūtras are of Āpastamba, Hiraṇyakeśin, Baudhāyana, Gautama Vaśiṣṭha, Mānava and Vaikhānasa (the Nārayana, Viṣṇu cult is mentioned in this text).

Beside these there exists the Pariśiṣta with some of the Gṛhya Sutra texts. It means the appendix connected with.

The Sūtra stage is considered as Smṛti. The Vedas are Śruti. The main divisions are :

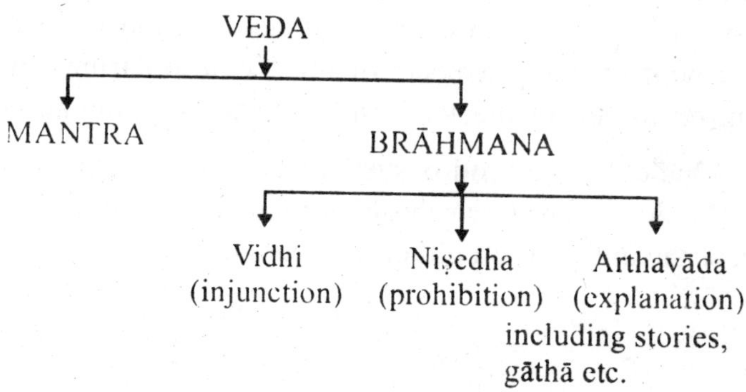

The Vedas are presented in different ways (forms) : Samhitā *i.e.*, words in combination, Pada Pāṭha, *i.e.*, words are taken singly, Krama Pāṭha, *i.e.*, words are repeated in the text etc. Attached to each veda, there is Anukramani, *i.e.*, index. Also an index of the 'many gods' exists which is known as Bṛhaddevatā.

The complexities of Śrauta and Gṛhya rituals are analytically described in some manuals which are called Prayoga, Viniyoga, Paddhati and Kārikā. Functionally they are guides containing the course of action, methodology of the rituals and the function of the priests involved etc.

In this study the Śutras relating to other areas of knowledge have not been taken into account (mentioned) except the treatises (Sūtras) of philosophical literature, which rank as Nyāya Prasthāna.

Although it is true that 'each text reflects the needs and questions of its own time', it should also be borne in mind that religion and philosophy are not any detached development form other areas of development, the reciprocal influence marks the profound achievement of certain period of time in the cultural history of any nation. The Upaniṣads are not systems of philosophy, but gradually the six systems developed accepting the authority of the Vedas. It is very strange that the acceptance of the vedic authority does not mean the acceptance on the existence of God or acknowledgement of every aspects of the Vedic doctrines, it was required to accept the leadership of the Brahmin class.

One of the authrodox systems is Sāmkhya, upon which the Bauddha and Jaina systems were based, they did not accept the authority of either the Veda or the Brahmin caste.

DARSHANA

The philosophical ideas accommodate various speculations of differing opinions. As Prof. Macdonell puts it :

The beginnings of Indian Philosophy which are to be found in the latest hymns of the Ṛgveda and in the Atharvaveda are concern with speculation on the origin of the world and on the eternal principle by which it is created and maintained. The Yajurveda further contains fantastic cosmogonic legends describing how the Creator produces all things by means of the omnipotent sacrifice, with these Vedic ideas are intimately connected and ineed largely identical, those of the earlier Upanisads.........

Altogether nine systems may be distinguished, some of which must in their origin go back to the beginning of the six century B.C. at least, of the six system which are accounted orthodox no less than four were originally atheistic, and one remained so throughout... The boldest philosophical speulation and conformity with the popular religion went hand in hand, to a degree which has never been equalled in any other country. Of the orthodox systems, by far the most important are th pantheistic Vedanta, which as continuing the doctrines of the Upanisads, has been the dominant philosophy of Brahmanism, since the end of the Vedic period, and the atheistic Sānkhya, which for the first time in the history of the world, asserted the complete imdependence of the human mind and attempted to solve its problems solely by the aid of reason. (History of Sanskrit Literature, pp. 327).

It is difficult to elucidate the fundamentals of philosophy as there is no agreement among the philosophers with its concepts.

The Sanskrit equivalent to philosophy is 'darshana'. It is derived form the root dṛs meaning 'to see', and the word seeing includes perceptual observation, conceptual knowledge and intuitional experience. The term darśana implies dṛṣṭi 'vision' (the sight, the search/pursuit = a vivid concept), draṣṭā 'subject' (the seeker, an actor/an individual), and draṣṭavya 'object' (the purpose/the goal, which has to be achieved).

Therefore, darśana is not just any concept or theoretical view of a social group systematised following an analytical procedure. It is considered as the gateway for illumination, its knowledge is the path to wisdom. It is concerned with the ultimate truth, the nature or reality.

Traditionally the āstika philosophy's metaphysical position is regarding soul, nature, cosmology and final goal. The aim is to interpret the nature of ultimate reality.

The Āstika Nāstika division is as follows :

The Sāmkhay, Yoga, Mimāmsā, Vedānta, Nyāya, Vaiśeṣika = Āstika and the Bouddha, Jaina, Cārvāka = Nāstika.

The word āstika means 'it exists', the word nāstika means 'it is not' (na-asti). Also there is the Tāntrika mata. All these conflicting philosophical systems have some basic agreement (except the Cārvāka mata) - an earnest longing for realisation of truth, a strong belief in karma, which causes the cycle of endless birth and death, i.e., transmigration, an aspiration for mukti (liberation/emancipation) and the conviction that the way out is to transcending the state of mind (dhyāna, samādhi).

The Six Systems of Āstika Philosophy

Sāmkhya : The logical analysis for a systematic account of the process of Cosmic evolution applying reason.

Yoga : The means of attaining the transcendental knowledge, the psychological process of knowing. The means of union with truth (unity of Jivātmā and Parmātmā).

Nyāya : Mainly concern with the means by which knowledge may be obtained. It is an enquiry with the means of knowledge.

Vaisesika : The knowledge of the properties of essential things, enquiries into the object to be know, the process of knowing the characteristics that distinguishes the eternal objects : dravya, the viśeṣa of dravya.

Mimāmsā : Consolidated conclusion of the method to interpret the Vedic injunctions : the action enjoined, the potency of action; also dealing with the pramāṇa, the purport of the words.

Vedānta : Deals with the later part of the Veda : interpret the knowledge (revealed) contained in the Upanisad regarding 'brahman' 'ātman' and 'jagat'.

Here are Some Quotations

'Each philosophy is the conceptual elaboration of an ultimate metaphysical standpoint.' (T.R.V. Murti, Concept of Philosophy, p. 55). 'By philosophy we mean the human quest for the ultimate reality, the knowledge of the ultimate truth.... when we approach the knowledge of ultimate reality by means of reason we have 'philosophy' when we do it by way of faith, we have Theology.' (R. Panikkar, Concept of Philosophy p. 59). 'The object of philosophy is to gain the perfect and complete knowledge of the truth, which is no mere aggregate of all possible views and experiences of the objective world, but an immediate experience of reality in the transcendental conciousness.' (Swami Prabhāvānanda and Frederick Manchester, The Spiritual Heritage of India, p. 211).

All the systems have some logical arguments, psychological explanation, metaphysical principles and religious attitudes. Also no system is the work of any individual. The systems were developed over the long period of time. Several ideas and thoughts when crystalised and took a shape it was synthesised as a system. To establish supremacy, each system puts forward some arguments refuting the objections raised bv others.

Sāmkhya

The Sāmkhya system and its sūtras are attributed to the muni (sage) Kapila. Like most of the philosophical system its aim is also to put an end of sufferings. The sufferings are classified as ādhibhoutika : extrinsic (external causes), and ādhidaivika : the natural (caused by the supernatural elements) and ādhyātmika : the intrinsic (caused by bodily on mental infliction).

This system establishes two things : the demarcation of matter and sprit on the one hand and on the other proclaims that the end of Samsāra (transmigration) depends on the recognition of the right (sharp) discrimination between these two : the matter and sprit.

The term that refers to matter is Prakṛti. The prefix 'pra' means pre, before, *i.e.*, eternally existent. The root 'kṛ' means 'to make'. So kṛti gives the meaning 'work', 'making'. Therefore, the term Prakṛti signifies primal substance. It is explained that out of which everything is evolved. This primal substance is 'acetana' *i.e.*, devoid of consciousness, but having the gunas of sattva, rajas, and tamas. Which imply existence, action, and restraint, which are characteristics of this manifested world (phenomental world).

Prakṛti is unknown cause, beyond the comprehension of human intelligence. To activate the unconscious source material for world appearance (production) *i.e.*, the manifestation including physical and biological existence some conscious agency is required.

The sprit, Sāmkhya puruṣa is the pure consciousness, signifies the animating principle by which the motion starts- the phenomenal world appears. Its features are : prakāśa (existence/manifestation), pravṛtti (action/tendency), and niyamana (restraint/control).

There is an inter play between the two : prakṛti and purṣa. The sṛṣṭi *i.e.*, the process which involves sthiti and laya; in other words in this process rhythmically recurs sustenance and dissolution.

The term puruṣa is explained as 'purisete' *i.e.*, puri meaning the citadel, sete meaning 'remains/ resides/dwells'. The Sāmkhya conception of puruṣa reminds us the Ātman-Brahman concept of the Upanisad. In the Veda we have found the theme of creation. Later the Gita speaks of the concept 'bīja pradah pitā', the father of all creation. Sāmkhya puruṣa is the mover, the 'spiritual agency'. It is cidrūpa (cit = consciousness, rupa = form).

Mahātattva

The first evolutes are :

Mahat = Cosmic intelligence or 'apparatus'.

Buddhi = contains guna, the reflected intelligence of the self.

Antahkaraṇa 'the mind stuff'.

Ahamkāra = the sense of individuality, the sense of agency, the ego.

Manas : Panca indriya = five organs of perception

Panca indriya = five organs of perception *i.e.*, Jnanendriya = five organs of action i.e., karmaendriya

Tanmātra Mahābhuta

Man = 'to know' = perceiving through the indriyas : cakṣu, srotra, tvak, rasanā, ghrāna, vāk, upatha, pāyu, pani, pāda. (*i.e.*, perception comes through the indriyas).

Tad = 'that', tanmātra means 'thatness = sound, touch, colour, (sight/vision), touch, smell corresponding to sabda, sparśa, rupa, rasa, gandha.

Bhu = 'to exist'.

Mahābhuta = great elements *i.e.*, ,earth, water, fire, air, ether, corresponding to kṣhiti, apa teja, marut, vyoma. The manifestation (world appearance) occurs in conjuction (compounding) with these twenty four categories.

In the Devi Sūkta of Ṛgveda we have come across with the notion of all pervading energy. The sāmkhya Prakṛti gives the idea that Prakṛti is the epitome of primordial source material pulsating in conjuction with the Purṣa. Later development in Tantra culminating the idea of Mother goddess Umā. This word appears to be the juxtaposition of the three sounds containing in the Praṇava mantra 'OM' = A U M.

The Upaniṣadic teaching concludes that the Ātman is verily the Brahman.

Man is an amalgum of several koṣa : the annamaya koṣa (the gross body), the prāṇamaya koṣa (the life breath), the manamaya koṣa (the will and desire), the vijñānamaya koṣa (the thoughts and ideas) = this is man's phenomenal existences, for which an individual passes through gathering experiences through his/her sense in the present life and the life to come.

The Puruṣa resides within, the Self, which is the unchanging, undying witness. According to Sāmkhya the right knowledge *i.e.*, (svarupajñāna) – the correct meaning of this self has to be understood.

The Sāmkhya gives an analytical exposition of its dualistic view, *i.e.*, the reality of the Pursṣa and the Prakṛti. The conception germinated in the Śvetaśvatra and in the Kaṭha Upaniṣads. Two theories are prominent : (*i*) Sat-kāryavād - the potential existence of effect in the cause itself. (*ii*) Parināmavād - the constant change in the conditions and collocations, while the reals remain unchanged.

According to Sāmkhya this world of experience is real. Prakṛti is the ground of all psychical and physical world. The mind is a product of Prakṛti, so it is not an intelligent doer, it is an instrument of Puruṣa (the Self). Finite knowledge is the product of mind, finite experience is gained through the mind by a process of reflected intelligence of the Self.

Prakṛti is not a force on energy, it is the material basis, it is the name of unknown, it is alinga, avyākta. The evolution in the organic and inorganic matter is of gradual unfoldment. The characteristics of physical universe is movement and of psychological universe is restlessness, so a static ground which holds them on is assumed. The conscious principle, the eternal invisible, suddha (pure), buddha (conscious/ intelligent), mukta (liberated/unbound) Puruṣa is the underlying base. This is in a nutshell the metaphysical conception of Sāmkhya.

In Sāmkhya the plurality of selves is accepted. The self is consciousness itself. The life force (prāṇa), the bio-motor-energy is the aspect of buddhi. Each buddhi with other evolutes forms an organic whole, a microcosm. Buddhi is the organism with which the past karma is active and ignorance is associated. Ego is 'the psychological unity' of an empirical being. 'Each life history has its linga', *i.e.*, the subtle body which retains the senses and psychy, reborns with puruṣa as an individual. The inner puruṣa is the Sākshi (witness) not bhoktā (affected). It is compared with a crystal which seems to be coloured by any colour in proximity.

In Sāmkhya view the bhoktā is the Jīva. The feeling of pain and suffering is due to the association of intelligence and the objective world. When the svatta guna dominates the individual gets Knowledge. Rajas gives rise to desire, restlessness and action. Tamas causes avidyā and jādya.

This system of thought gives little importance to the performance of Vedic rites. It views mukti as the removal (destruction) of individuality. Its concept of evolution suggests a continuing unfoldment (development) linking all forms of life, plant, animal and man.

Sāmkhya accepts the Yoga method for controlling senses, removing vāsanās (desire/hankering), developing calmness and balancing Citta. The discipline of yoga is incorporated in this system.

There is no written document to the founder's teaching. The extant text is Sāmkhya Kārika of Isvarakṛṣna. There are commentaries composed by Gauṛapāda (700 AD), Vācaspati Misra (1100 AD) and Vijñāna Bhikṣu (in the middle of 16th Century). The Sāmkhya view of three gunas has been accepted by all other systems. In the Pauranic literature the conception of Purṣa and Prakṛti have been converted into the male and female principles.

There are two distinct lines in Sāmkhya : Seśvara and Niriśvara, *i.e.,* acceptance and non-acceptance of Iśvara (God). The Sāmkhya systems primary effort is to analyse the meaning of the world of phenomenal existence.

Yogadarśana

The word yoga means 'yoking', joining the mind. The means and methodology of concentration are expounded in the Yoga Sūtra of Patanjali (200 BC).

The definition of yoga is 'citta vṛtti nirodha' The ultimate aim of yoga is 'svarupe avasthānam' (returning to the core). The definition indicates 'stilling the waves of citta'. This is an experimental discipline. There are four Padavinyāsa (aspects/dimensions) as follows :

Samādhipāda = the goal

Sādhanapāda = the discipline

Vibhutipāda = the self evident signs of progress

Kaivalyapāda = the attainment/the sublimation.

Through the rigorous discipline and earning power the aspirant proceeds towards the ultimate goal. The gradual unfolding in Patanjali's viewpoints :

(*i*) **Samādhipāda** : The goal of the Yogadarśana is to obtain wisdom (prajña), which dawns upon in samādhi (the state of complete absorption).

(*a*) On the one hand to realise the meaning of Pariṇāma, the real nature of Prakṛti which is magnanimous, diverse multiplicity.

(*b*) On the other hand the true nature of Puruṣa which is unity, non-action.

(*ii*) **Sādhanapāda :** The discipline is to polish (sharpen) the sense perception to make it ready for divine perception. Our ordinary waking life (jāgrata avasthā) *i.e.*, our mind is sense bound, we are wide awake to the world outside. The sense perceptions are mediate perceptions. The yoga practice is an attempt to remove mediacy.

(*iii*) **Vibhutipāda :** The attainment of yogic power, the state of full control.

(*iv*) **Kaivalyapāda :** Svarupe avasthānam.

At the beginning the aspirant needs to do the vahiranga sādhana. The purpose of yoga practice is to restrain the mind and to make it steady. The primary practices (discipline are yama and niyama.

Yama

Ahimsā (non-injury in body mind and action), āsteya (non-stealing), brahmacaryā (sexual restraint), aparigraha (non-acceptance of anything more than necessary).

Niyama

Suddhi (cleanliness of body and mind), tapas (austerity-control of body-mind-speech = kāya, vāk, manah samyama), svādhyāya (study of scriptures), Iśvarapranidhāna (meditation on Iśvara also the ritual performance), pratipakṣha-bhāvanā (replacing selfish motive, desire for possession, wish to overpower etc. by contemplation and good thought to pacify the mind thinking that I have taken a vow/shelter to yoga-darśana).

veloping Certain Attitudes

Maitri (friendly attitude), karuṇā (kindness/compassion), uditā (feeling happy in other's happiness/feeling sympathy other's sorrow) upekṣhā (indifference to mundane things= saya vairāgya, indifference to other's vices).

Also conscious effort to be made to create opposite ought wave when selfish emotions come. Constant practice th śraddhā (*i.e.*, faith and conviction) gives strength and gour. Even at one stage it is necessary to still noble oughts.

The antaranga sādhana comprises samyama = dhyāna-ārana - samādhi (trayamekatra samyama). The discipline within (mental practice).

Other necessary practices are : āsana, prāṇāyāma, atyāhāra.

sana

Convenient posture (sukhāsana) helps concentration. ntrol of food and drink is also recommended. Parimita ara (moderate eating) makes the body free of fatigue and rest decay, makes the body strong and graceful.

āṇāyāma

Control of the prāṇa, it brings rest and peace to the ind's activity. There are three aspects in this activity : halation, exhalation and pause respectively, Pause means ssation either in the lung on after exhalation.

atyāhāra

Controlling the outgoing tendency of mind, it is the ithdrawal or restraining of the sense from their functions.

Now the body movement is stopped *i.e.*, firmly sea on, breathing is controlled, organs are controlled then outgoing tendency of mind will be automatically chec and turned inward = parama vaśyatā indriyanam.

We have already mentioned the other three : dhāra dhāyāna, samādhi.

Dhāraṇa

Fixing the mind in the Centre within, contemplating the name and the quality of the chosen deity, repeating chanting the OM mantra. These three conditions necessary requirement for dhāraṇa to be successful.

Dhyāna

Continuity of the same wave, concentrating on c particular object mentally to be repeated or thought.

Samādhi

Absorption in one thought is samādhi, when t concentration is so intense that the mind is lost in ecsta absorption. There are two categories : samprajñāta a asamprajñāta.

It is mentioned that in samprajñāta samādhi t knowledge of the object remains. The unfoldment of t mysteries of life occurs. Occult powers may be obtain The eight occult powers (aṣṭasiddhi/vibhuti/yogavala) ar animā, laghimā, vasitā, vyāpti, mahimā, isitva, prakām and kāmāvasāyitā.

The cessation of samprajñāta samādhi leads asamprajñāta samādhi, when there is no object knowled It is being one with consciousness, the intuitive insight, ıer mental mode, that is called 'kaivalyaprāpti' being one ith the reality: 'pratyakṣam' - direct experience. In this anner the description is given.

The word yoga has several meanings in several contexts. ›metimes it means the method, sometimes it means the ıion or joining. Patanjali's Yoga Sutras describe the method attaining Samādhi. The Sūtras teach and explain the nature mind, the gradual steps for restraining the mental operation ıd eradication of its exhibitive habit. All mental operations e of the nature of pleasure-pain and ignorance (here norance means the sphere of afflications). The memory eans retention of experienced objects.

In Yogadarśana the right knowledge is not enough, adication of vāsanas and Samaskāra are necessary. It firms that there is an inherent desire for freedom in man gether with the desire for life enjoyment. One can reach e state of full control *i.e.*, complete giving up or being ›sireless by discarding the attainment of vibhuti (the yogic ›wer) - then he is in the state of vasikāra. It means who ıs no craving for mundane enjoyment (viz., women, food, ealth, power or heaven) and who is indifferent to the power yoga, even scriptural enjoyment. When the citta vṛtti ›ases completely then only the Puruṣa shines with glory.

It is said :

yogena yoga jñātavaya yoga yogāt pravartate/
yo paramattvastu yogena sa yoge ramate ciram//

Patanjali's Yoga Sūtra gives guidance to eight discipli- ›s for regular practice. The text has four divisions the second ıvision explains the method.

The Sūtras and the Bhāsya explain the meaning of amsāra, Kāraṇa, Prakṛti, Puruṣa and Viveka. The Yoga philosophy is dualistic in its characterisation of Puruṣa a Prakṛti.

The Mahābhārata and the Bhagavadgitā consider th the Sāmkhya and Yoga are not different except one refe to the theory and the other to practice.

The Sāmkhya gives detail analysis of the meaning the world of phenomenal existence referring the reality the Superme Spirit. Beyond the sense perception ext sensory psychic perception is possible that is the assertic of Patanjali's Yogasūtra. The yoga can transform o personality. As the ultimate aim is 'svarūpe avasthānar being in true nature, elaborate explanation is given. Sever words are used to indicate the condition : 'svarūp pratisṭhā; 'citiśaktiriti'. This word 'citi' indicates the sparkin (vicchuraṇa) of consciousness, as it is in feminine form ar it is compounded with the term 'śakti', it signifies 'spanda (pulsating), although pure consciousness is 'aparināmi' *i.e* no transformation, changeless (niskṛya, nirvikāra), howeve this is the yoga outlook *i.e.*, aparinami can have sandan.

According to the Tantra aparināmi svarupa can b 'parināmi spandita Śaktirūpa'. According to Vedānt 'caitanya' (pure consciousness) is "viśuddha bodha', n transformation ever, and spandan or parinām is in the spher of Māyā. (The explanation is understood form Prof. Govind Gopal Mukherjee's elaborate discussion, Nibhodhata Jul 2001).

Yoga admits that every soul is divine, its true nature i considered to be bounded in physical form of body-min complex of empirical existence (microcosom).

The 'I' is nothing but a bundle of experiences an memories. It is a mistake to identify the real (the self) wit the instrument *i.e.*, the mind, buddhi etc.

Citta comprises of manas, buddhi and ahamkāra. Manas records the sense data, buddhi is the discriminative faculty, ahamkāra is the 'I'-sense. The term aham means I and kāra is an agentive suffix. Percerption is a vṛtti, a thought wave.

The Puruṣa is not subject to either happiness or misery. The cause of suffering is the desire for sense gratification,, emotional satisfaction and strong attachment to them. So it is necessary to control and restrain such desire. It is necessary to eradicate the latent 'potentialities' (samaskāra), the inherent tendencies which are carried over form the past lives. It is the result of Kārmic law in individuals life which remains in the unconscious level, this rooted tendency moulds individual's character. Also the external world causes agitation in the mind. Therefore it is necessary to make conscious effort for balancing the mental modification.

Yoga admits that every soul is divine and body is the vehicle for divine experience. Patanjali accepts Iśvara but yoga-Iśvara is not the creator.

There are five fold afflictions (kleśa)

avidyā = ignorance

asmitā = egoism

rāga = attachment

dveṣā = hatred/aversion

abhinives = clinging to life

Other afflictions are sickness, lazyness etc.

The five stages of citta

pramurḥa = ignorant (concentration on attachment)

kṣhipta = wild (concentration on passion)

Vikṣhipta = unsteady (flicking from one to another)
ekāgra = one pointed (steady concentration)
nirodha = cessation (mental modification stopped)

There are five fold vṛtti (process/modification) of citta

pramāṇa = valid knowledge
viparyaya = false knowledge
vikalpa = imagination
nidrā = vacant mind/sleep
smṛti = memory

All these tendencies are innate, with these we lean towards Samsāra (affliction) or mukti (liberation). The right knowledge is enlightenment. For obtaining such enlightenment, thought wave must be controlled, thought waves must be stopped.

Nyāya

The Nyāya Sūtra of Gotama is the treatise of Nyāya system. There are several commentaries on the Nyāyasūtra. The first one was written by Vātsayana (450 AD).

The Nyāyasūtras describe a process for establishing knowledge. Nyāya is a pramāṇa śāstra 'science of correct reasoning'. It adopted a method of critical analysis. The Nyāya and Vaiśeṣika both offered analytical investigation into the world of experience.

The Nyāya gives a theory of knowledge. There are four conditions to be fulfilled in an enquiry of knowledge:

Pramātṛ : The subject (the cogniser of the cognition).

Prameya : The object (to which the process is directed).

Pramiti : The cognition.

Pramāṇa : The means of knowledge.

The Pramāṇas are :

Pratyakṣa : Perception (including intuitive perception).

Anumāna : Inference.

Upamāna : Analogy, comparison.

Śabda : Verbal testimony (scriptures, trustworthy person's words).

The origination of knowledge is due to sāmagri, the collocation or combination of sense activities, contact with the objects by both intellectual and physical contact knowledge or cognition is produced.

This system provides a process of sixteen means for establishing knowledge : (1) pramāṇa, (2) prameya, (3) samasyā (problem/doubt) (4) prayajana (purpose), (4) dṛsṭānta (example), (6) siddhānta (conclusion/tenet), (7) avayava (body), (8) tarka (confutation/logic), (9) nirṇaya (ascertainment/ the result of investigation/findings), (10) vāda (discussion), (11) jalpa (controversy), (12) vitaṇḍā (cavil), (13) hetvābhāsa (fallacy), (14) chala (pretence), (15) jāti (futility), (16) nigrahasthāna (the point of disagreement).

Through the above mentioned process correct knowledge can be obtained and through the correct (right) knowledge niśreyasa can be achieved. The effort should be looked upon as a kind of worship. Together with the intellectual effort (reasoning), moral and spiritual discipline should be maintained by developing humility, self surrender and devotion to Iśvara.

The Nyāya method has been accepted by all other systems even by the nāstika Bauddha.

VAIŚEṢIKA

The Vaiśeṣika system has been crystalized in the Vaiśeṣika Sūtra of Kañada. From the theory of viśeṣa the system is know as Vaiśeṣika. Its psychology describes the innate connection of Soul with the internal organ of thought - manas.

The system describes dharma : the nature of padārtha (categories/entities), they are dravya (substance), guṇa (quality), karma (movement), samanvaya (aspect of generality), samavāya (relation/togetherness), abhāva (negation/ want of something), viśeṣa (perception of diversity particularity).

According to this system there are two sources of knowledge :

pratyakṣa (perception), and anumāna (inference).

It admits five cognitive senses which direct knowledge by perceptual process. Manas though a sense organ can come in contact with transcendental nature. There is an unknown factor 'Adṛṣṭa', which is the cause of the phenomenal world, it also connects the body and the soul. Due to the contact of the inner soul and the manas - senses, the objects through the senses, we get pleasure and pain.

The Vaiśeṣika admits the existence of Iśvara as the agency of world order. The above mentioned seven categories compose the universe; individuality is particular where change is inevitable, generality is universal which is changeless. These two are inseparable, that is the theory of samayāya. The relation between the substance and quality also is inseperable. Substances (dravya) are independent : pṛthivi (earth), apa (water), tejas (fire), vāyu (air), ākāśa (ether), kāla (time), dik (space), ātman (soul), manas (mind).

The Vaiśeṣika gives exposition how to look at the process of the vast ever changing multiplicity of the sound colour forms of the phenomenal world. The enquiry begins with the findings of the basic realities of nature, knowing the similarity and differences, characteristics, combination composition and transformation, the truth is known.

The world experience comes through the sense data which is natural and subject to space, time and causation. The Ātman is characterised as : prāṇa (breath), apāna (descending breath), nimeṣa (closing of the eyelid), unmeṣa (opening of the eyelid), jīvana (life), manogati (movement of the manas), indrīya (senses), sukha (pleasure), dukha (pain), icchā (desire), prayatna (effort/volition), these are the signs = linga of Ātman. The characteristics of Consciousness is awareness. It exists in empirical existence, the subject.

The Ātman and manas are connected and produce all experiences of knowledge, feeling, memory, willing etc. The correct knowledge makes one dispassionate and removes moha (delusion).

The physical and moral orders of the universe imply a controller, an intelligent agency. There is no visible body of Iśvara, but Iśvara is a Being and the cause of the 'manifest world'. Iśvara is existence, consciousness, and bliss. Individual self is separate form Iśvara.

The Nyāya-Vaiśeṣika speak of parispanda ('molecular movement') which produces the effect form the cause, there is a time relation between them; this concept is known as 'kāray-kāraṇa-bhāva' (the cause and effect relation).

Perception/Cognition = Knowledge

The indrīyas (sense), manas (mind), ahamkāra (ego), buddhi (intellect), these are the instrument, acting as follows:

(*i*) senses are excited by object contact,

(*ii*) mind receives the sense data and forms into percept,

(*iii*) ego refers it to the self,

(*iv*) intellect forms the concept = perception occurs.

In any cognition the inner organ is reflected in Puruṣa, and the intellect is modified. The Puruṣa's reflection in intelligence is called knowledge. Perception can be of two types : savikalpa and nirvikalpa. The Nyāya-Vaiśeṣika validate savikalpa, *i.e.*, perception with mental analysis and synthesis-'psychological stage'. (S. Das Gupta, History of Indian Philosophy, pp 338).

All the systems consider samsāra is painful, knowledge gives freedom form the bondage. Ātmapuruṣa resides in every jiva. The Puruṣa is free and untouched by impurity. The Sādhan (strive) is for realisation of the nature of the Puruṣa. The knowledge is na-asmi/na-aham *i.e.,* not me/not I. This knowledge results form yoga sādhanā.

Vairāgya (non-attachment) and viveka (discrimination) can not be developed by controlling emotional activities only. By practicing dhyāna citta becomes samāhita (calm), vāsanā (impulsive tendencies) are lapsed and an impersonal attitude develops. When sattva guṇa prevails mind becomes thoughtful, calm and balanced.

In yoga philosophy vairāgya is attributed as passionlessness, desirelessness and samāpatti which means that the mind is in balance.

MĪMĀMSĀ

The word mīmāmsa means investigation, inquiry, also it refers to the meaning conclusion,–'a consolidated conclusion/reasoned conclusion'.

The Mīmāmsā Sūtras of Jaimini is a compilation of thoughts and ideas of one school, the date of compilation may be around 200 B.C., its famous bhāṣya (commentary) was written by Sabara (probable date 57 B.C.).

These are the foundation of Purva-Mimāmsa. Kumārila Bhaṭṭa wrote his famous work in three volumes of Sabarasvāmi's bhāṣya known as 'Ślokavārttika', 'Tantravārttika' and 'Ṭupṭikā'. Traditionally it is believed that he was an older contemporary of Sankarācārya. Kumārila Bhatta's disciple Prabhākara (AD 650) had some disagreement and gave exposition differently.

The subject matter of Mīmāmsā, is the 'Investigation of the nature of Duty' (Ganganath Jha, Purva Mīmāmsā, pp. 187). The connotation of duty is dharma, dharma as a ritualistic performance with a practical purpose.

Dharma as an act of performance of yajñā and other religious duties. We experience life in the external world, so dharma to be actualised in action which will lead man to happiness.

The Mīmāmsā gives exposition of the earlier portion of the Vedas so it is called Purva-Mīmāmsā. It explains the meaning of karma enjoined in the Veda so it is known as Karma-Mīmāmsā also.

There are three categories of karma :

Nitya : The Sandhyā.

Naimittika : Ceremonial performances.

Kāmya : Performance of sacrifices for attainment of some beneficial results.

Moral codes and all injunctions are to be maintained. The compulsory and occasional karmas have deeper significance. By performing the prescribed rites in correct manner, observing obligatory duties and abiding by moral laws man can attain welfare here and perpetual happiness here after. This is the import in the Karma section. 'Apurva' the unexpected welfare and happiness can be attained in this life by doing dharma. Therefore, accordingly following the Vedic injuctions, sacrificial rites, ceremonial rites and every day rituals etc. have to be performed. The Mīmāmsā also explains those actions which are completely prohibited.

The Ṛk, Yajus and Sāman together are called Trayi Vidyā. The Ṛk mantras are for the invocation of the deities. They are recited aloud. The Yajus mantras are to be pronounced during the offering in fire. The Sāman mantras are for singing at the time of fire sacrifices.

The Veda itself is 'Brahman in the form of sounds, *i.e.*, word/expression (S. Radhakrisnan, Indian Philosophy Vol. 2, p. 428). The Veda is selfexistent, uncreated. The eternal knowledge is contained in the Vedas.

The Vedic contents are :

Vidihi : Injuction

Mantra : Hymns/praise

Nāmadheya : Names

Niṣedha : Prohibitions/forbidden acts.

Arthavāda : Rules of rituals.

The Mīmāmsā emphasises that with śraddhā (faith), bhakti (devotion), tapas (austerity) the Vedic rites to be performed. Otherwise 'we incure' pratyavāya/aparādha (wrong doing).

Yajñā is the main. The link between the action (performed rites) and its result, *i.e.*, the 'Apurva'. There exists and unknown power (adṛśya śakti). The sound 'Om' is the symbol and it is identical with Brahman.

The obligatory and occasional karma have deeper significance. By properly performing the prescribed rites, observing obligatory duties and abiding by the moral laws one can obtain happiness. The scheme of right living is dharma. The injuction (codana) is the sign of dharma. The term codana signifies command, inspiration form within, the dicates which ought to be performed.

UTTAR MĪMĀMSĀ

The Uttar Mīmāmsā, *i.e.*, the later inquiry is concerned with the Upaniṣadic philosophy, the Jñānakāṇḍa of the Veda. The philosophical aspirations are synthesised by Bādarayana in the Brahma Sūtra.

Ācārya Śankara identifies Bādrāyana as the Sūtrakāra. Rāmānujacārya, Madhvācāry, Vallabhācārya and Baladevācārya give the authorship to Vyāsa. In general the time of compositions of the Upaniṣads and the Brahmasūtra according to the Indian scholars, should be between 500 BC to 200 BC.

The system of Vedānta darśana is developed on this treatise. The Upaniṣads are the ending portion of the Vedas. The Sanskrit word for end is 'anta'. So it acquires the name Vedānta. In 555 sūtras the Sūtrakāra presented a summary of the Upaniṣadic ideas, it is an attempt for systematisation of the teaching : a synopsis of the contant of the Upaniṣads.

As the main topic of discussion is Brahaman and Its manifestation, the embodied soul, the sūtras are known as Brahma Sūtra. It is also known as Śāriraka Sūtra because it deals with the self embodied in the śarīra (body).

There are four chapters in this treatise. The first one deals with the nature of Brahman. Its relation to the world and the individual soul. The second chapter discusses different theories. The third explains the Sādhanā, *i.e.*, the ways and means of gaining Brahma-Vidyā (tattvajñāna). The fourth speaks of the result of attaining the Brahmavidyā.

The title of these chapters :

The first chapter is 'Samanvaya' = the coherent interpretation of Śruti (different Upanisadic teachings).

The second chapter is 'Avirodha' = showing the similarity and agreement among different views.

The third is 'Sādhana' = the means.

The fourth is 'Phala' = the result.

The main theme or the central teachings of the Upaniṣads are :

Self enquiry (svarūpa Jñāna),

developing detachment (vairāgya),

knowledge of discrimination (viveka) = to see things in its proper perspective,

realisation of identity (ātma-brahma jñāna) = the knowledge of fundamental unity.

The goal of Brahma Sūtra is to provide the knowledge of Brahman (Brahmajñāna). Brahman is changeless (avikarī). Bādarāyana accepted both the ideas of indeterminate intelligence held by Bādari, Kāśakṛtsna and Oudulomi (the idea that Brahman is 'nirviśeṣa cinmātra'), also the other opinion that Brahman is determinate personal Lord, 'Saviśeṣa'.

To obtain the knowledge of Brahman it is necessary to purify the instrument, *i.e.*, the body mind complex. The Yajñā and austerity are recommended for the higher three castes. The weaker sections (women and śudra) should make effort for receiving Lord's grace. The absolute is beyond the reach of human mind. The symbol (pratika) is recommended for ordinary people.

Following ethical discipline the aspirant should make himself fit. An aspirant should have required qualifications for studying philosophy.

The qualifications are :

(*i*) Nityānitya vastuviveka = the power of discrimination between eternal and non-eternal, *i.e.,* the sense of seeing (judging) things in their proper perspective. Eternal means the unchanging reality while non-eternal refers to the changing world.

(*ii*) Vairāgya, *i.e.*, detachment,

(*iii*) 'samadamādi sādhana sampat' = moral preparation, *i.e.*, sama, dama etc.,

(*iv*) 'mumukṣatavam' = loging for liberation.

The seeker of truth, the enquirer of knowledge should have no hankering of objects in ordinary life. Darśana (philosophy) means the 'vision of truth'.

The following maxims can be deduced :

Reasoning should be considered subordinate to intuition. Brahaman is the material and efficient cause of the Universe, so the relation is non-different (ananya). Brahman is uncreated (anādi). The soul is eternal.

There are several commentaries of Brahma Sūtra and there are differences (among them) of opinions.

Gauḍapāda

Gaudapada's Mānḍukya Kārikā is an important exposition which has systematised the non-dualistic view of the Upaniṣads. The unity of self in three stases of waking, dream and sleep is explained. The consciousness that remains constant is permanent and it is the witness of individual's existence.

In the waking state we experience the physical world (samsāra), the experience in the dream state has no contact with the external world, in suṣupti what persists is pure consciousness. The 'relative nature of phenomental world' is explained. The idea of creator God, bondage, misery of the samsāra sweep away when the realisation comes. It is necessary to make constant effort by spiritual practices to attain the higher phase of consciousness.

The spiritual discipline as the literature suggests, is the unfolding of latent divinity of human beings through conscious effort.

The Commentators

The well known commentators are : Śankara (788-820), Bhāskara (1000 AD), Yādavaprakāśa (1000 AD), Rāmānuja (AD 1140 - ?), Keśava, Nilakanṭha (AD 1278 - ?), Madhava (1238 AD), Baladeva (1725 AD), Vallabha (1479 - 1544) and Vijñānabhikṣu (1600 AD), Nimbarka (13th century).

ŚANKARA (788-820 AD)

Śankara wrote commentaries on the Upaniṣads and the Brahmasūtra. His interpretations established Advaita Vedānta. He gave much importance to the fitness for studying Vedānta philosophy. The Vedānta instructions (sādhan) includes the qualifications mentioned before. It also give the methodology:

(*i*) Śarvana (it is necessary to listen to the interpretations of the purport of the Upaniṣads).

(*ii*) Manana (application of reasoned arguments to strengthen conviction).

(*iii*) Nididhyāsana (engaging in the yoga process of concentration and meditation which brings realisation).

The self is unchangeable, all other events are passing appearances. The cognition of world appearances go when the knowledge dawns upon. Ajñāna means the non cognition of the nature of the phenomenon world. The phenomena are temporary and relative in existence. Cit is pure consciousness. It manifests itself, Cit is not an object of consciousness.

Due to the natural tendency of human mind the transcendental and empirical are confused. Our cognitive mechanism is limited by space time. We are unable to grasp the ultimate reality, it is related with the world of plurality (nāma-rūpa). The world appears to be mysterious. We try to conceive Brahman with the logical mode of thinking. But Brahman is existence in its entirety. It is not a substance nor it is limited by space time relation.

satyam jñānam anantam brahma/

The absolute is knowledge itself (jñānam), not the subject of knowledge.

nisprapanca sadātmakam//

The World (Jagat)

The world existence in space time causality is relative. There are three levels :

Pāramārthika : The higher plane,

Vyavahārika : The empirical existence,

Pratibhāsika : The illusory existence.

The higher plane can be reached by making effort, the experience can not be described. Śankara uses the word 'anubhava'–it can be felt, it is a kind of illumination, felling bliss and delight. The time-space bound empirical life and events are at the level of vyavahārika.

The structure of mind is such that we congnise the pluralistic universe, it appears like that, which is illusory. The world is based on the absolute, the phenomenon world is not the eternal absolute. Advaita Vedānta explains that our emotional life is dominated by two opposites of love and hate. It is reflected in our mental attitude.

We are indifferent to the unknown things. We want to avoid which is not pleasing to us or which is painful. We dislike those things - this attitude is dveṣa (hatred). Whatever we desire, wish to posses or obtain we like, we like those. We feel happy, it appears to us desirable, commendable (priya). Bṛhadāranyaka Upaniṣad says that everything is dear to us in relation to the self. Our self is extremely dear to us. For the sake of enjoyment and gratification we superimose (adhyāsa) on wealth, son, wife etc.

False imposition has to be discarded. By meditation and yoga one can be established in Ātman (self), that brings real happiness. Knowledge, love, wisdom, pleasant feelings all are accrued in the psychical plane. When mental modifications are blissful, mental condition is constantly satisfied (nitya prāpta avasthā), that mental condition is defined as 'rasa'. And it is said that Brahaman the source of 'rasa' can be realised in the state of such sublimated psyche.

The meaning of knowledge in this context is - the comprehension of the eternal nature of Brahman and the nature of the objects of name and form of world appearances.

By applying the objective method of analysis it has to be differentiated/discriminated : the characteristics are asti (existence), bhāti (manifestation), priyam (attractive), nāma (name) and rūpa (form). The three - asti, bhāti, and priyam are the nature of Reality (Absolute = Satyam = Truth) - the eternal Being (= Sattā). This is the farthest extent that human intellect can cognise and express in words : Sat Cit Ānanda = existence (Being = asti), intelligence shines (= bhāti), and bliss, priyam (= ānada).

The other two refer to the nature of the world.

The core of Advaita Vedānta (*i.e.*, the central thesis):

there is nothing other than Brahaman, the ultimate Reality, the self is Brahman;

the true knowledge is the experience of oneness, the experience of otherness is fragmentary, illusory;

the whole manifested and unamanifested world of things are the creation of mind (imagination = kalpanā), it is explained as 'citta spandana' (vibration of the citta);

the Brahman can not be known by the discrimination alone;

we can conceive Iśvara as the cosmic self who is the creator, sustainer as well as the dissolver;

the ultimate truth cannot be grasped by the mind of a human being because it is limited in nature (Kaṭh Upanisad 1.3.34).

'jivabrahmaikyam suddhacaitanyam prameyam tatra eva vedāntānām tātparyat'/

The essence of Vedānta are - the identity of empirical and universal self, its nature of pure intelligence, which has to be realised.

The objective method is mentioned. The subjective method is analysing the three states of consciousness : jāgrata, svapna and suṣupti. In suṣupti the pure intelligence remains constant as witness. The subjective method is for understanding the total mind of an individual. The purpose is to transcend the mind into a higher plane where emotion, thought, will and cognition are integrated. In the words of Swami Vivekananda : 'when a mind is fully developed it is linked up with the universal mind' (Works 11,13).

At this juncture a brief outline of some other concepts may be useful. An individual = Mānava.

Man is an amalgam of physical body, vital dynamism, psychic principles and the eternal Puruṣa.

One may have right knowledge through pramānas, can recognise the causes of desire, but eradication of desire does not come easily. Knowing the true nature of things, knowing that worldly things and relations have relative existence and individual is circumstantially entangled, this sense in the proper term is very difficult to arise.

Though we may understand that this is the basis of human suffering, we are unable to detach ourselves. But the mind can be controlled if the functions of mind is understood properly.

The Functions (Modifications) of Mind

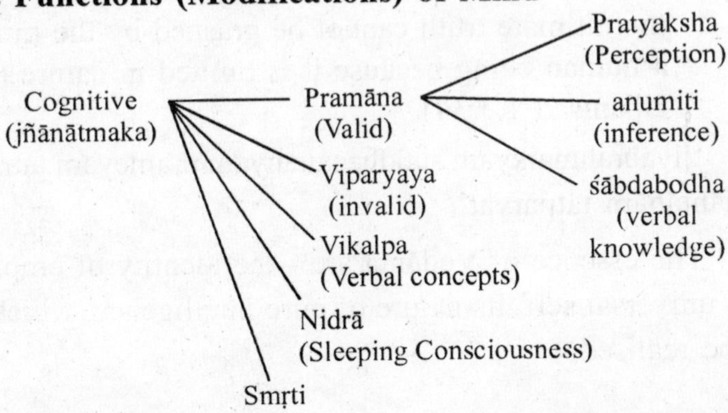

In the Ayurvedic (medical science) context mind's functions are looked at as follows :

(*i*) the mind is capable of knowing truth,

(*ii*) its function is to direct and control sense organs and to receive impressions,

(*iii*) buddhi (intelligence) makes judgement.

From the Vedas, Upaniṣads (Ṛk, Yaju, Bṛhadāranyaka, Aitareya) the term antahkaraṇa can be found.

Two views can be deduced form the philosophical literature : mechanistic and psychic.

The mechanistic view describes mind as a connecting link between the sense organs and the soul. The Nyāya, Vaiśeṣika, and Mīmāmsā subscribe this view. The other view is that the mind functions as the agent of the soul. The Sānkhya, Vedānta and Pātanjala hold this view.

The process or the functioning of mind is difficult to explain. In this context the word 'antah' means inner and the word 'karaṇa' means instrument. However, the description of anthakaraṇa in Indian psychology is like the following :

antahkarana includes

Manas	Buddhi	Ahamkāra	Citta
(collecting faculty receiving impressions)	(intelligence-decisive faculty, makes decision, judgement)	(ego-asserting faculty,asserts)	(storing faculty restores)

Our own feeling of love, hate, anger, fear, envy, anxiety etc. can surely be analysed by ourselves, but how we become aware, how memories are stored can not be analysed, can not be explained either, as nerve sensation. The process or the functioning of mind is not very simple to explain. The total mind is described in its different states :

Jāgrat : The walking mind is conscious,

Svapna : The dream state, and

Suṣupti : The deep sleep, in both the subconscious is alert.

The other condition 'turīya' the highest (the super conscious) is also recognised.

The conscious mind receives current impressions. In the subconscious state the impressions are stored, it carries impressions form the past (samaskāra). The conscious mind gets influence form its environment. As mind works through the nervous system, when the nerves are tired the mind becomes dull (tāmasika), when the nerves are overacting the mind is very energetic (rājasika), when the nerves are in balanced state, working in regulated manner, the mind is calm and peaceful (sāttvika). So purity of body is essential as mind works through the nervous system.

The nervous system could be strengthened by physical and mental purificatory method : food, exercise, regulating thoughts and emotions. The quality of mental habit can be changed by strong will. The primary quality of will is conviction on our own self.

It is the natural tendency of mind to get confused with the empirical existence and the existence in its entirety. It is a common phenomenon of finite mind, though it is assured that through the right understanding the course of life can be changed.

Physiological Concept

Organic body is made up of the (*i*) gross elements, (*ii*) the life organs and (*iii*) the subtle body.

The subtle construct of organic body - the seed of the body (dehavīja) : the sukṣhma/linga sarīra (bhutāsraya).

The other elements are karmāśraya : (*i*) five organs of perception, (*ii*) five organs of action, (*iii*) five prāna (vital instruments), (*iv*) the mind (*v*) the intellect. The unconscious life force is the support of human life, the sense organs and physical apparatus are sustained by prāṇa. But there is something within the body-mind complex mechanism which binds together experiences, perceptions, and memories. This is the background of storing.

The outer organs operate on objects present to them, mind is the internal organ which coordinates them, receives sensation. The mind is connected with both organs of action (motor impulses) and organs of intellection (sensory impulses). The organs of action are known as 'karmendriya', and organs of intellection are known as 'jñānendriya'.

The eyes, ears, skin, nose and tongue are the sense organs through which sensory impulses are received by the mind. The intellect governs our sight, hearing, touch, taste, smelling and thought waves. Intelligence is reflected in the mind through the generating power of that, which remains in the permanent background. In a nut shell this is the mechanism of perception (cognition). Besides this there are some instinctive urge, *i.e.*, inherent impulses or emotions (instinctive desires) : self preservation, self expression, sex impulses, urge for company and urge for knowing.

These aspects of mind : cognition (perception), emotion and volition can be controlled. Iṛā the sensory nerve currents,

Pingalā, the motor nerve currents can effectively be synthesised by breathing exercise.

The effects of breathing exercise : regulates the respiratory system, nerves become strong, and feeling of relaxation prevails.

The mind is always receiving impressions and the restless thought waves come. Mind's waves need to be concentrated by making the habit of thinking for one thing for some time. But putting (concentrating) mind on material objects does not yield mental upliftment. Puruṣa is the witness, the eternal being. So is the aim to concentrate on the eternal Purusa to obtain real happiness and bliss. Basically human beings aspire for happiness, want to become immortal.

In the Aitareya Upanisad it is said that the self gains knowledge through the mind (awareness = sajñā). The mind perceives through the sense organs (perception = ājñā). From attentive perception arises discriminative knowledge (vijñāna). The resultant form is intelligence (prajñāna). This can be developed by making effort, study. (A.U.3.5.2)

According to Sāmkhya-Yoga, and Nyāya-Vaiśeṣika the sense organs are prāpyakarī, *i.e.*, they are causing perception. But Advaita Vedānta says that the mind itself apprehends, perceptual knowledge differs due to the instruments (eyes, ears etc.) Perception is direct immediate knowledge. According to Śamkara true knowledge can not be expressed in language. Consciousness is the only reality, it has no beginning and no end. It is the basis of empirical knowledge.

The idea is that mind is material and it can not be dissolved, so it is necessary to control the ever flowing current of mental modes, the distraction and passion (vikṣhepa and kaṣāya). The nature of mind is to flowout, it goes to every directions. That has to be checked if one is desirous of knowing (wants to realise) the true nature of the self.

The first step is to rise above the dualities of anger and hatred, also pleasure and pain. This results in equanimity. Which develops concentration. It is necessary to have a positive attitude, *i.e.*, satisfaction and cultivation of śraddhā. Then practise concentrating on a subtle object. By following this method, mental modifications gradually subside, citta ceases to act, no outgoing aspect is left, the flow becomes uninterrupted, this is the state of meditation. At this stage the realisation of oneness comes. That is knowledge, it comes intuitively, not through intellectual argument. It is experience. Brahman is knowledge, that which has to be realised. Brahman is indefinable, beyond the reach of words.

Individual Self

The meaning of Sākṣhin, Jīva and Ātman is difficult both to explain and to understand. The relation of Ātman and the empirical psychological self is mysterious, we do not understand because our cognitive mechanism has limited capacity. Individual consciousness is the representation of Brahman but how that representative status could be articulated with logical explanation?

The relation of consciousness in a body is finite, the conscious experience develops in time. But Ātman is not limited by space-time. Ātman is not linked with individual 'life-history'. Individual ego is a complex unit, it is in a frame of body with organs and phenomenal character is attached to the body, sense, mind and sense objects.

Ātman covered by upādhi (limitation) is the bhoktā (enjoyer/suffer) and kartā (doer/agent). The real self

(Sākṣhin = witness) is free. The enjoyer and doer is the Jiva, so is the possessor of fruits of action (karmaphala). The empirical existence is bound down by manas. The relative reality of empirical existence bound by space-time-causation is linked with religious obligation, merits/demerits, law, command, injunction, prohibitions and prospects. All these are from the point of view of identifying the self with the impermanent body, physical limit, individual consciousness covered by upādhi. Jīva is ignorant of its divine origin, so it is subject to samsāra, *i.e.*, subject to three guṇas. Brahman is the substratum of all soul of all creatures. This is in a nutshell the explanation given by the philosophical literature and supposed to be the accepted opinion of Śamkara.

The Sākṣhin is the eternal consciousness, it cannot be identified with the Jīva. Jiva is the empirical ego. According to Śamkara the different states of the individual self are as follow :

In the waking condition (jāgrata avasthā)–perception of the world through the mind and senses : in the dream (svapna avasthā) condition — the mind only is active. In the deep sleep condition (suṣupti)–there is no activity either of the mind or the senses, the real nature (prajñā) shines. The individual self is the part of the Universal self. The individual self has cognitive, emotional, conative experience and it is the Sākṣhin. Pancadasi (x.ii) gives a beautiful analogy : nṛtyaśālāsthita dīpah. It is like the lamp on the stage, when the acting is going on the light is on, when it is over still the lamp gives light.

The pure consciousness, the eternal Being is formless, operating in the Cosmos, when the same is operating through an individual organism is known as Jīva-sākṣhin. The Jīva has two aspects, one way the doer, actor, enjoyer and the other aspect is prajñā, remaining in real nature, the unchanging pure consciousness, the witness (Sākshin). Sometimes the word Intelligence refers to the same. The Absolute and its reflection refers to 'vimba prativimba bhāva'.

Knowledge

The term 'jñāna' means knowledge. All knowledge imply—an object, a subject, and a process; in other words, the cogniser (the subject), the act of cognition (the process), and the thing to be cognised (the object).

There are some fundamental notions :

Knowledge is considered as a quality of the self, which is manifested through the mind, due to the mental modifications and consciousness knowledge occurs. The mental modification is the field and consciousness is the illuminating factor. The means of acquiring knowledge are called 'pramāṇa'. They are perception (pratyakṣha), inference (anumāna), comparison (upamāna), verbal testimony (śabda), presumption/implication (arthāpatti), nonexistent/contrast (abhava), and tradition (aitihya).

According to Nyāya perception-inference-comparison-verbal testimony/authority are the means of acquiring knowledge. Mīmāmsā adds presumption/implication. While Vedānta adds one more - contrast/nonexistence. Finally, tradition is included by the Paurānika as a means.

Perception : It comes through the sense organs (eyes, ears, skin, nose, toung). The mind is the mediator. Perception could be-sense perception, mental consciousness and yogic intuition.

Inference : It occurs on seeing the sign of the object. It could be primary (=vidihi), secondary (=arthavād), or higher inference.

Comparison comes with similar things, that also gives knowledge.

Knowledge can be obtained form the śāstra. Also can be gained form the knowledgeable authority.

Śabda as a Source of Knowledge : Every word has a meaning which is conventional. The meaning is known through popular usage, grammar, dictionaries and gesture. A word with its form and content denotes both individual (vyākti) and genus (jāti). These two are interrelated, *i.e.*, a substance and its quality together (samavāya).

The verbal cognition occurs through recollection. A sentence meaning is understood through the interrelated-independent-fit constituent words, in other words the sounds combination occuring in a structure.

The words of the Ṛṣis are known as adṛṣṭārtha, *i.e.*, assertion relating to the invisible world. The Ṛṣis received them in intuitive perception, those are recorded in the Vedas as they desired to communicate out of joy, for the posterity their words are preserved.

The words of reliable persons are known as authority (āptopadeśa).

Knowledge (jñāna) exists where there is a manifestation of ātman (life). According to Sāmkhya, Yoga, and Advaita Vedānta the Ātman is consciousness itself. Knowledge includes both cognition (anubhava) and recollection of previous experience (smṛti). The effect of knowledge (result) is knowing the essence. This is the object of knowledge (svarūpajñāna). In other words the real nature of Ātman (self-life), this is the concept of Cit (as it is explained that it is nothing but consciousness). The nature of the Self is existence, without the life principle every thing is meaningless at the empirical level. The brain, *i.e.*, the nervous system representing the body, the mind representing the mental functions (thoughts, feelings, doubts, determination, memorisation, resolution, capacity for accomplishment, intelligence, retaining impressions and so on); the mind absorbs consciousness and consciousness is reflected in mind. All activities and contact with the external objects by its own modes (cittavṛtti) and through sense perception. In combination of all these formalize the concept of existence, *i.e.*, the concept of Sat.

The Vājasenaya Samhitā and Upaniṣads recognise mind as a psychical entity not merely as a physical sense organ. And harmony that which life is seeking, *i.e.,* Ānanda (bliss in the form self knowledge) = Equanimity.

It is already mentioned before that to Śamkara true knowledge can not be expressed in words, it is beyond human language, he has used the term 'anirvacaniya'.

It should also be borne in mind that 'svarūpa' is neither physically nor psychologically existent. Because life is not identical with chemical compound though arises from the combination. Human beings can only conceptualise the existence of transcendental nature of selt within, it is impossible to pinpoint on the experimental desection. The meaning of transcendence is to go beyond the empirical, endeavouring to link up with the Universal, intuitive flash of identity of individual Self with the Whole. In philosophical term it is the identity of Puruṣa with Brahman.

The Object

The realisation of the divine transcendenal state of human beings and relatedness of cosmic existence is the object of true knowledge.

As the object is independent of perceiving, conceiving and rememberance, it is necessary that the value system available in the culture ought to be followed, to be practised in our empirical existence of this phenomenal world. The Vedic worship, *i.e.*, prayer, performance of sacrifice and other rituals to be carried on. We live on the plane of diversity so it is absolutely necessary to maintain the ethical principles in its throughness in both individual and social lives. These are the prerequisite for spiritual growth and development.

The Yoga system of Patanjali provides a methodological process. The spiritual discipline as the literature suggests is unfolding the latent divinity of human beings through the conscious effort.

There is a difference between the psychological 'self' me, the empirical ego and the 'Puruṣa' the pure eternal self, the divine 'Ātman'. Every object is known as it has a form and a name. The form is mental, the name is expressed in word. In this context the object is 'svarūpajñāna' its knowledge is perceived, cognized and apprehended through the mind, in other words can be realised (be conscious about) through the mind.

Summary

At this point we may summarise that Dharma to be understood as the Vedic obligation; a household should perform yajñā, lit up fire, to maintain Dharma the caste and āśrama duties should be fulfilled. Brahmajijñāsā, the higher enquiry for universal truth gives stress on reason and self discipline. A person able to make buddhi (reason) as a means who is pure in thoughts, words and deeds would be fit for such enquiry.

The philosophical investigation is known as Nyāya Prasthāna. The philosophical inquiry is vicāra (application of reason), a rational inquiry regarding existence. The knowledge comes intuitively in the state of 'samādhi' for which 'sādhanā' (yogic discipline) is a must.

The idea of four stages of life is significant, it indicates a gradual development of understanding : affirming the worldly values of human aspirations, the mature minds approach to the higher goal. The stage of learning, the stage of social obligations, domestic obligations, then gradually shifting to the spiritual investigation, asceticism and renunciation were the ideals of Vedic tradition.

The other characteristic features found are - the idea of many gods in the Samhitā, the one source, the one impersonal power in Upanisad and the stress on reason and discipline in the philosophy for realisation of Upanisadic ideals. The devotional attitude to a personal god is emphasised in the Paurānic teaching.

In the tradition of philosophy the two significant issues are recognisable - one regarding the language and the other regarding 'oneness', the identity of One with multiplicity.

DIFFERENT STREAMS

The Vedas are the source of Indian religious and sublime philosophical thoughts, they are repository of higher imagination. Over the course of time, the two currents become visible, the Vaidika and Tāntrika, though they do not always run in parallel. Sometimes they are mixed up and converge and sometimes they diverge but they are found concurrent.

Scholars have Differences of Opinion : Some say Tantra has a Vedic origin, some think it is pre-vedic.

However, it is true that both Vedic and Tāntric elements are infused in Indian religious thoughts, ideas and rituals.

The word Tantra mainly refers to Pancopāsanā, the five systems of Hindu religion, which cover the worship of Viṣṇu, Śiva, Śakti (Devi), Ganapati and Surya. Accordingly the sects are named : the Vaiṣṇava, Śaiva, Śākta, Gānapatya and Saura, and each has its own tantric text.

In Kāsikāvrtti the word Tantra is derived from the root 'tan' meaning to spread. So it seems that originally the term meant a technical text of any religious system.

Besides the Pancopāsanā, there exist Buddhist and Jaina tantra texts. The noticeable characteristic of Tantra lies in its spiritual practices (sādhan padhaties) which include purification (suddhi), elevation (uddhāra) and regaining consciousness (caitanya). The Tantric mode of ritual worship is quite distinct.

The original Vedic concepts and practices gradually incorporated ideas, concepts and practices form other traditions. The Smṛti texts show the rise of the theistic tradition, though the devotional attitude may be traced in some Upaniṣads. But its strong focus is established in the Smṛti texts. Scholars have the opinion that it was during the reign of the Guptas (320BC to 500CE) that the worship of several Gods and Goddess gained prominance within the Vedic tradition, there gradually developed the devotional attitude to a personal God or Goddess.

The two Epics, the Mahābhārata and Rāmāyana, and the Purāṇas are classified as Smṛti together with the Dharma-śātras. All these texts communicated the ideals, aspirations, traditions, philosophy, religious rituals and customs of the Hindus for generation after generation.

The followers of Smṛti are known as Smārtas; they perform Pancopāsanā. Those who perform Vedic rituals are Śrautas. Besides these there is the Atimārga way.

However the devotional attitude is common to all these systems. The Pancarātra, Pasupata, Śākta and Gānapatya are generally considered as Tāntric systems.

PANCARĀTRA

Pancarātra literally means five nights, but is difficult to define. It is a 'rahasya āmnaya', i.e., a mysterious knowledge taught by Viṣṇu to Brahma in five nights. It is referred to as Ekāyana, the only way to salvation. As it contains doctrines and rituals, it is an Āgama, and as it spreads ('tanoti') spiritual knowledge, it is a Tantra.

Pancarātra is associated with Vaiṣṇavism, as the central deity is Nārāyaṇa. In the Satapatha Brāhmana, Nārāyaṇa is identified with the Vedic Puruṣa. The Pancarātra is mentioned in the Mahābhārata.

The Bhāgavatas are worshippers of Vāsudeva-Kṛṣṇa and Kṛṣṇa-Gopāla; in actual fact, the deities Nārāyaṇa, Kṛṣṇa and Viṣṇu are one and the same.

The Vaikhānasa is sourced form the Taittiriya sākhā of Kṛṣṇa Yajur Veda. The temple worship of Tirupati follows this tradition.

These three main streams with their various sects are all Vaiṣṇava. The most important sects are the Śrivaiṣṇavas in Tamilnadu, the Gauḍiya Vaiṣṇavas in Bengal, the Vithobhā worshippers in Mahārasṭra, the Rāmāyits in North India, and the Puṣṭi Mārga in Western India. In the medieval period many saints preached the path of devotion. One of them was Merābāi whose sādhanā was rāgānugā bhakti.

Lord Viṣṇu is worshipped in different forms in these traditions, and the mode of worship is of mixed type with elements of Vaidika, Paurānika, Smārta and Tāntrika.

Pancarātra Agama prescribes self surrender (prapatti), while Vaikhānasa Āgama emphasises Vaidhi bhakti and ritual worship covering all other means needed for the path of devotion including pujā, arcanā, yajñā etc.

The devotional (bhakti) tradition is characterised by an emotional outpouring. This tendency is not solely restricted to the Vaiṣṇavas, but is the hallmark of all later systems as well, whether they are Vaiṣṇava, Śaiva, Śākta or Gānapatya.

The Development of Vedic Viṣṇu

The concept of the Cosmic Puruṣa (Supreme Self) was gradually transformed into Avatara Kṛṣṇa through the Paurānika idea of Ananta Śayana Padmanābha and Śankha-Cakra-Gadā-Padma dhārī (holding the conch, discus, mace and lotus in four hands), Viṣṇu descends as Kṛṣṇa, promising that whenever it is necessary to establish dharma He will manifest himself as avatāra (in descended form) murti.

Mention has been made of the Vāsudeva worship in Pāṇini's Aṣṭādhyāyi (500 or 600 BC), Patanjali's Mahābhāṣya (200BC) and in the Pāli Canon (100BC). Kṛṣṇa is referred to in the Chāndogya Upaniṣad; in the Mahābhārata he is the king of Dvārakā, while the Harivamśa supplies information concerning Vṛndāvana Kṛṣṇa.

ŚIVA

Rudra the dreadful in Ṛgveda become Rudra-Śiva in the later Vedic literature, Śiva meaning 'the benignant' (a term used by Prof. Bhāndarkar). Though the concept of Rudra originally referred to fear and awe, gradually the sentiment of love, tenderness and auspiciousness developed with the idea of Rudra Śiva, which is evident in various Śaiva systems of later days. The auspicious Śiva was known by several names. Through the Veda, Upaniṣad, Rāmāyana, Mahābharata and Purāṇas Rudra Śiva become Mahādeva.

The devotees of Śiva are mentioned in Patañjali. The word Pāśupata is mentioned in the Mahābhārata. There is inscriptional evidence since 943 AD, the existence of four branches of the Pāśupata system.

The Vaiśeṣika Sūktakār Kanāda, Bharadvāja of the Nyāya school and Haribhadra, a Jaina author of the Gotama school, were all followers of Śaiva systems. The 7th century Chinese traveller Hiuen Tsiang mentioned Śaiva temples in his book. He witnessed a large number of Śaiva ascetics in Benares. The copper plate evidence also gives information about the existence of Kāpālika or Kālāmukhas form the middle of 7th century in Mahārāsṭra.

Information can also be gathered form literature : Kālidāsa, Subandhu, Bāna, Śri Harṣa, Bhaṭṭa Nārāyaṇa, Bhavabhuti and many others wrote Śiva stuti (praise) at the beginning of their works.

The Linga and the Śiva-Purāṇa are the most important Śiva Purāṇa. The other main Śaiva texts are known as Āgama or Tantra. Like Vaiṣṇavism, Śaivism is also characterised by the devotional attitude.

The temples of Kedārnath in Tehari Garwal district, Paśupatināth in Nepal, Somnāth in Kathiawar, Viśwanāth in Kāshi (Benares), in Kashmir, in Rāmeśwaram and in Bengal prove that Śiva worship was prevalent in India form time immemorial, even in Pre-Vedic time, as Śiva figurine found in Mahenjodāro testify. In the long course of time the idea of Rudra Śiva Paśupati gradually become Maheśwara Mahādeva, Naṭarāja, Śadāśiva.

In Śamkara's commentary on the Brahma Sūtra, reference is made to the Siddhantas (or Śaivāgamas). It is believed that the source of the Āgama is the Lord himself.

In Śamkara - Vijaya of Anandagiri, six Śaiva sects : Śaiva, Rudra, Ugra, Bhaṭṭa, Jangama and Pāśupata are mentioned. Each of these schools developed in a different part of the country. The Āgamic Śaiva in Tamilnadu, Pāśupata in Gujarāt, Pratyābhijñā in Kāshmir and Vira Śaiva in Karnātaka. Śaiva devotees can be classified into different classes. Each school contains both ascetics and lay devotees, while some devotees do not belong to any particular sect.

Śiva the Lord of the Yogis[1]

He dissolves all diversities. He holds the Triśula : the three prongs of his spear are the symbols of vairāgya (renunciation), jñāna (knowledge), and samādhi (absorption). With these the demon of ego in its gross, subtle and causal bodies (symbolised as Tripurāsura) can be destroyed. He rides on Nandi the Bull representing dharma with four feet: truth, purity, kindness and charity.

Śiva murti is adorned with snakes, for the cobra symbolises death. Lord Śiva is known as Mṛtyunjaya the conqueror of death. So to him the cobera is an ornament. Again in the Tantra Śāstra a coiled serpent represents the basic energy of living beings (the microcosm), as well as the cycle of time in the macroecosmic sphere. Śiva is the 'master of time and energy'.

He is the lord of the stage; He is Naṭrāja, producer of the continuous process of creation, preservation and

1. Hindu Symbology and other exays, Swami Swahānanda.

dissolution. In one hand the lord holds the Damaru (rattle drum) which sounds the Nādabrahma of evolving creation. Another hand shows abhaya mudrā, promising shelter for who seek refuge (śaranāgata). The moon in His forehead is the candra mandala of the yogis. Śiva's three eyes see the past, present and future. They are the Sun, moon and fire or Iḍtā, Pingalā and Suṣumanā. He is trampling the Dwarf (apasmāra), *i.e.*, ignorance (ajñāna) and ego (ahamkāra) which make us lose our balance and consciousness. Apasmāra is trampled upon by the Lord for the good of devotees. Gangā (the river of nectar) is in the Sahasrāra. The Lord's body is balanced on one foot, while the other foot is lifted in the catura (or lalita) pose. His waist is in twist pose and He is dancing - which symbolises eternal evolution and movement. The dance also suggests the Lord's fivefold actions, of creation, preservation, destruction, embodiment and release. He spreads the veil of illusion, but also removes the veil. The flame surrounding Him (agnisikhā), dissolves the world after the cycle of time, it symbolises the process of destruction.

TANTRA

The Tantra texts are believed to be revealed texts. They take the form of a series of dialogues between Śiva and Pārvai. (In Vaiṣṇava Tantra the dialogue is between Bhagavān Viṣṇu and Lakshmi).

In the Śaiva Tantra, Lord Śiva is the Guru and Devi Pārvati is the receiver. In the Śākta Tantra Devi (Śakti) is the Guru and Śiva Himself receivers wisdom form Her. In the Tantras Śiva and Śakti are difficult to separate.

The Tantra and Purāṇa in general follow a similar format : the pancalakṣhana, *i.e.*, the creation, dissolution, worship, attainment of power (siddhi) and union. These are the subject matter under discussion. The difference is that the Purāṇas elaborately describe the mythological (aspect) elements, whereas the primary focus of the Tantra texts is on the spiritual discipline (sādhanā); they give details on rituals in the fashion of the Brāhmana texts of the Vedic tradition. The Tāntric text is divided into four divisions (pāda = feet) : Vidyā, Kṛya, Yoga and Caryā (or Yoga, Caryā Upāya and Siddhi).

There is a wide variety of modes of worship in the Śaiva tradition. Paurānika devotees worship with mantra and bhakti, Tantrika devotees worship with cakra, mandala while Kāpālika, pāśupata devotees follow the outer path.

The Tāntrika religion first appeared in Northern India. Important early manuscripts are found in Kāshmir and Nepal. From there it spread over the vast area of the Eastern part of the country and then penetrated to the South. By the eleventh century the Tāntrika elements were absorbed into Hinduism, especially in the Vedic-Paurāṇic system, if not the Vedic Śrauta tradition.

KĀSHMIR ŚAIVISM

The Kāshmir Śaiva sampradāya beginning with Vasugupta who flourished in c875-925, is commonly known as Trika. According to tradition Vasugupta found some verses inscribe into rock. This inscription is the main source of his Śivasūtra which laid the foundation for the Kāshmira Śaiva darśna.

The literature of this system is divided into three categories : Āgama, Spanda and Pratyābhijña. The Āgama is regarded as revelation. The word literally means to come down, to appear. Vasugupta's Śivasūtra is considered as Āgama Śāstra; it contains the monistic philosophy of the system. The Spanda elaborates the doctrines, while the Pratyābhijñā contains the philosophy, rituals and yogic practice.

One of the important texts of Kāshmira Śaiva mata is the Tantraloka of Abhinavagupta (C975-1025).

Briefly the purport is as follows :

According to the Trika system or Tarikāsana (Kāshmira Śaiva system) the concept of Puruṣa-Prakṛti in Sāmkhya and Brahman-Māyā in Vedānta are of a dualistic nature. According to Trika a single Reality has two aspects : the Transcendental, which is unmanifested, and the Immanent, which is all-pervading. Though the logical mind can not reach pure monism, in samādhi realization comes. The Sāmkhya Puruṣa is inert, but the origin of action (creation) is due to the association of Prakṛti, though no reason is given for such an association. Vedānta postulates an intelligent agent, the designer of the cosmic law and movement, but no explanation is given for the initiation of movement. Trikāsana's explanation is that the original substance alternately acts and reacts. The period of action is sristikālā, the phase of manifestation (Ābhasa), while the phase of rest is pralaya (dissolution) *i.e.*, the period of reabsorption of manifested phenomena.

The Sāmkhya system postulates two independent realities: spirit, which is conscious and matter, which is unconscious.

Vedānta postulates one ultimate reality : Brahman and considers the manifest world a mere appearance.

The Kāshmira system contends that the manifest world is real : it is just a phase of one reality. The process of evolution of the pure consciousness is vi-varta (to turn around) in Vedānta, while in Kāshmira Śaiva it is described as Abhāsa (shining forth/glow). The ultimate reality : Parā Sambit i.e., Supreme Consciousness is personified as Parama Śiva, the deity (cidānanda rūpa). His universal desire (Icchā) and universal intelligence (Jñāna) are the source which is described as Caitanya where everything lie. The changless Being-Consciousness-Bliss (Sat-Cit-Ānanda) is Niṣkala, Nirguṇa which is beyond time and space beyond the mind's conception. The epithent Niṣkala means 'no parts', while Nirguṇa means 'no attributes'. It can only be realised in samādhi (turīya avasthā) i.e., in the state of spiritual illumination (transcendeal meditation).

Manifestation means appearance. The process of cosmic evolution is explained in terms of Śivatattava and Śaktitattava. Śiva is the Cit aspect and Śakati is the Ānanda aspect. These two are called Aham and Idam i.e., the subject and object. Aham means I and Idam means this. The word Śakti is derived form the root sak 'to be able'. Śakti is explained as energy, power of Śiva, personified as the Mother of the universe *i.e.*, the procurer. These two can not be separated, they are eternal and unproduced.

There are several tattavas : Sadāśiva, Iśvara, Sadvidyā etc. The tattavas form Śiva to Sadvidyā are considered as suddha tattava *i.e.,* of pure category.

Sadāśiva : Manifestation = the notion of Being with the power of desire i.e. Icchāśakti, a concept which can be compared with the Vedic idea of 'eko yam bahu syam'.

Iśvara : Deification of the divine glory.

Sadvidyā : The pure knowledge of the dual relationship and unity of Aham and Idam.

The concept of Māyāśakti is also postulated; it casts a veil on the pure category and thereby being both mind and matter under its spell. However, in this system the concept of Māyā is not a separate entity. It is latent, it is the limiting principle, the world of limited experience.

The contracting potency of Māyā is known as Kancuka. There are five Kancuka : time, space, desire, limited knowledge and limited power, *i.e.* Kāla, Niyati, Rāga, Vidyā, Kalā.

The five modes of Universal Spirit (Conscious Being) are Cit, Ānada, Icchā, Jñāna, and Kṛyā *i.e.*, Śiva, Sadaśiva, Śakti, Iśvara and Sadvidyā. Their qualities are nityattva (eternal existence), vyāpakattva (all pervasiveness), pūrṇattva (completeness/fullness), sarvajñāttva (full knowledge) and sarvakatrttva (all powerful).

The cosmos is outpouring the vibration of consciousness and the individual soul is nothing but the Lord i.e., the identity of both. In a nutshell, the above mentioned are the concepts of Trika. Spiritual practices and methods are described in Abhinavagupta's Tantraloka. The ritual includes yogic practice, nyāsa (imposition of mantra), mental worship, having the vision of triśula (trident) and external worship using a maṇḍala (symbolic digram).

At one time the Kāshmira Śaiva system was wide spread and influential in northern India.

The **Śaiva Siddhānta** is the prevailing system in South India. This tradition originated in the North and came to South through the Central part of the country during the Cālukya, Paramāra, Kalacuri, Cedi and Kākatīya reigns[1]. Though there existed the Tamil Śaiva cult, the Śaiva Siddhānta fused with it and established a temple culture

1. The History and Culture of the Indian People, Vol. 4, R.C. Majumdar *et. al., eds.*

with the patronage of Cola, Pallava and Pāndeya kings of the South.

With the recurring onslaught of the Muslims, the Kāshmira Śaiva religion faded away, but it was revived in the Tamil land as a dualistic system incorporating bhakti, *i.e.,* maintaining the distinction of human personality form the Divine personality. The ritual, doctrine and concepts provided by Śaiva Siddhānta are distinctly of dualistic nature. This system maintains three categories : Pati, the Lord with His fivefold actions already mentioned in the description of Naṭarāja.

Paśu, the bounded soul which is not suddha, but is subject to pāśa. Pāśa is the bondage, the fetters which are an indispensable condition of world existence.

As the term Trika refers to 'Three fold' *i.e.,* (*i*) the traid of three Āgamas : Mālini, Siddha and Nāmaka's authority considered as the main, (*ii*) it speaks of Parā, Aparā and Parāparā Śakti, (*iii*) there are three modes of knowledge which are explained in this system (abheda, bheda and bhedābheda), and there are the three streams of literature which have been mentioned previously : Āgama, Spanda and Pratyābhijñā. Siddhānta, which incorporated Tantric elements was a later development. So, the term 'siddhānta' means the 'established or conclusive view'.[1]

The southern Śaiva Siddhānta merged with the existing Tamil bhakti cult and it became a dualistic tradition. Naturally in any dualistic bhakti (devotion) system, rigid concerns of caste are not very strong, and this is the case in southern Śaivism. Although a class of priest known as

---

1. Śaiva Siddhānta Theology, Rohan A Dunmwila, P45.

Ādiśaiva (belonging to five Brahmin families) are qualified to perform pujā in Śaiva Siddhānta temples.[1]

The Śaiva Siddhānta follows the path of mantra (mantra mārga) worshipping the deity as Sadāśiva. There are 28 Tantras (ten Śivāgama and eighteen Rudrāgama) and Paddhatis (manuals) for domestic and temple worship.

The Lingāyat or Viraśaiva sect is prominent in Karnātaka. This sect opposes caste hierarchy and ritualistic worship, as well as the authority of the Vedas. Śiva is worshipped through the linga.

In Gujarāṭ and Nepal the ascetic path of Pāśupata Śiva tradition remains strong. Although the famous Somnāth temple was plundered by the Muslims several times, it survived the attacks. The famous Paśupatināth temple is in Kāṭmanḍu.

From the above mentioned systems we learn that it is the experience of suffering that awakens the human mind and lead it to aspire for release. Devotion is the gateway and earning it is the way to receive the Lord's grace. Intensity in the devotee is the parameter for staring out in religious life. Step by step progress depends both on physical activities and mental discipline.

The Śakti concept can be traced back to the hymn of the Ṛgveda. The idea of Umā-haimavatī appeared in the Upaniṣad. Gradually the Vedic mode of Śakti worship was replaced by the Tāntric ritualism of devotion to the Mother Goddess.

The tradition of Mahā Devi is prevalent in the Purāṇas, especially the Devibhāgavata Purāṇa and Mārkandeya Purāṇa (Devi Māhātmya is a part of this Purāṇa). The Mother

1. Hinduism, Gavin Flood, p. 169.

goddess can be worshipped in many forms. She is the embodiment of paradoxical qualities; some of her manifestations are beautiful and gentle and some are fierce and terrible. Śakti means power, the active principle, the 'primal energy'.

Those who worship Śakti are known as Śākta. Devi (Śakti) is the supreme, ultimate reality. Mahā Devi encompasses all, she is the progenitor (Savitṛ), sustainer (Dhātṛ) and absorber (Samhātṛ). She is caitanya (Consciousness) and she caste the veil (Māya).

The Kaula System

The term kaula means family or group. Basically there are four regional branches of the system known as Kaula. The northern Kaula worships Gughyakāli. The southern Kaula worships Sadaśiva and Tripurā Sundarī or Kameśwari. The Śrividyā tradition developed from this system. In the eastern Kaula Śiva and Sakti as Kuleśwara and Kuleśwari are worshipped. The Kāshmira Śaivism belongs to this Kaula, known as Trika System. In the western Kaula the Goddess is worshipped in the form of Kubjikā, she is identified with Parā Devi. It is significant that in the Kubjikā text the first mention is found of the six cakras. And the concept of kundali is associated with Kubjikādevi.

ŚRIVIDYĀ

The beautiful Goddess Lalitā (Tripurā Sundarī) in Tantra is the counterpart of Śri Devi or Lakshmi. Tripurā Sundarī is worshipped in the form of a Yantra or sacred diagram, the Śricakra, which is the tool of ritual in Tantra system.

There are two basic division in the Kaula system. The Śrikula is prevalent in the south while in other regions the Kālikula prevails. There are several texts in this tradition.

The most popular are the Saundaryalaharī and Lalitā Sahasranāma, both composed by Śankara. The tradition of Śrividya is followed by the members of the Śankara monastic system at Śringeri and Kānchipuram.

The basic principles of both the Śrividyā and the Kāshmira Śaiva texts are not much different. The Śricakra is the representation (symbol) of both the deity and the cosmos. The method of worship with body mind and speech *i.e.*, meditation, uttering mantras or japa, using sound, and activities (physical ritual) such as offering flowers, food etc. correspond to the supreme, subtle and gross aspects of Tantric practice.

Women are venerated in Tantric ideology, though they may not enjoy equal status in society. The Paurāṇic and Tāntric Devi is all powerful and Her power energizes women. In Nepal and Bengal the practice of virgin worship (the Kumāri pujā) is still followed.

Among these kulas there are distinct types of practices, known as the Daksinācara (the right-handed practice) and the Vāmācāra (the left handed practice). They differ in the use of ritual substances and in the rejection of brahmanical conventions.

The mother Goddess Durgā is the most prominent manifestation among the Paurānic Devis. While the other aspects of the goddess take precedence in the Tantras.

The Vedic Devis Pṛthivi and Sarasvati (Vāc) are still worshipped but Aditi, Usas, etc have lost their separate identity. The worship of Durgā, Kāli, Cāmuṇḍā, and Sarasvati is widespread throughout India. Goddess Śri as Lakshmi is a pan Indian consort of Viṣṇu. In the south Minākṣhi Devi at Mādurā and Kanyākumarī Devi are famous. Kumāri is the manifestation of Durgā. Her temple is at the very end of the land where the Bay of Bengal, the Arabian sea and the Indian Ocean meet.

There are several important (sacred) sites (Śakti pitha), Kāmrūpa in Assam, Jālandhar in Panjab, Uddyāna (or Hinglāz) in the far north west, Kālighāt in Bengal and Mīnākṣhī in Tamilnadu.

The Śrividyā tradition adopted Vedānta theology, as well as Haṭha yogic practices, and Kundalini awakening with its Saṭha Cakra or six Centres which is associated with western Kaulas Kubjikāmata. And this Devi is identified with Parā Devi, which shows its connection to the Kāshmira Śaiva tradition.

Thus the Tāntric ritual and Paurānic Vedic ideals were fused together in later times to become a pan Hindu feature. Except for the extreme left hand Tāntric practices, the Tāntric Kaula tradition cannot be seen as outside the pale of Brahmanism. The Kāpālika, Kālāmukha and Aghora systems followed the left handed practice, which is prohibited in pure Brahmanism. One the other hand the ritualistic installation of the murti is always done by following Tāntric procedures.

We may summarise the development of the four main systems forms of worship and of source materials in the following way :

Sources	**Viṣṇu**
Veda	Vedic Sūkta
	↓
	Vaikhānasa Pancanātra Bhāgavata
Purāṇa Tantra	↓
↓	
Hinduism	Pauranika Viṣṇu Combined with Tamil Bhakti

<u>Śiva</u>

Vedic Rudra

↓

Paurāṇika → Pāśupata, Kaula, Trika, Śaiva Siddhānta, Śaiva Siddhanta in South

Tāntrika → Kāpālika, Kālāmukha, Lingayat, Aghora

<u>Devi</u>

Vedic Devi Sukta

Vedic Goddesses

↓

Paurāṇika Goddess

Tāntrika

↓

Śrikula → Śrividyā

Kālikula → Kāli and other Forms.

The foregoing introductory description is an attempt to outline the main sources and the gradual development of various ideas and practices into the Hindu religion as we understand it today.

With this basic sketch we intend to unraval the core of some system's discipline in the next section.

SECTION 2

DISCIPLINE

In this section we will turn our attention to the recommended paths for spiritual progress (Sādhana).

In ordinary social life, human beings aspire for the acquisition of material wealth, name and fame etc. Material satisfaction varies according to the ideal set by the class or level to which one belongs, as well as the social environment and the psychic condition of the person. In other words, aspirations mostly grow and develop in the social context.

The socio-philosophical thinkers of ancient India set up four goals for human life : dharma (duty/right conduct), artha (wealth/legetimate earning), kāma (desire/fulfilment of worldly aspiration), and mokṣha (final aim, liberation).

For the peaceful and smooth maintenance of a society it is extremely important that the members should learn the ethical values and discharge fully their prescribed duties and obligations (Sadācāra). Sadācāra is acquired by following tradition. In normal situations, tradition provides a framework and moulds the mind, although there is no guarantee that ethical virtues will necessarily grow in individuals who follow tradition. It is believed that dharma is acquired by following tradition and social norms.

The pursuit of artha and kāma is also a natural aspiration. For the fulfilment of these aspirations, it is necessary to develop a certain discipline, with the aim of building character, elevating the mind, and moulding the psychic condition of the individual. It is believed that the psychic condition can be moulded by religion, as religion sets the objective of rising above self-centered material craving and recommends effective guidance for inner harmony. If, after reflection on one's life experience one is desirous of higher knowledge, that person can cultivate the recommended disciplines.

The Spiritual Discipline : Sādhanā

This term includes both the discipline and its methodology. It involves the interplay of man, his mind, his actions and the meaning of spirituality. So the idea of man in Indian thought, the structure of mind in Indian psychology and the meaning of spirituality in Indian philosophy and religion are interwoven.

Sādhanā means engaging oneself in a particular discipline and practicing a certain methodology.

Sādhanā involves these three :

1. **The Seeker :** An aspirant (sādhaka, bhakta, ādhāra, adhikāri).
2. **The Seeking :** Mārga (the way, the path followed).
3. **The Object Sought :** Bhagvān (the Lord, Devi, one's chosen Deity) ātman/brahman : by means of ātma or svarūpa Jñāna/brahama jñāna (self realisation/cosmic realisation).

Sādhaka means the aspirant who is making a conscious effort to realise the truth and is trying to fathom the meaning of life by studying the relationship between empirical existence and the world process, between the body and mind, between consciousness and mind. A sādhaka is willing to develop the divine qualities. He is searching for higher knowledge (parā-vidyā).

Sādhanā is not dialectical thinking.

The word bhakta mans a devotee who is emotionally attached to a specific ideal (form of God/Goddess/Saint).

The word ādhāra means the receptive vehicle - the body-mind complex, the instrument of the aspirant.

Adhikāri means (*i*) a deserving candidate for receiving higher knowledge, (*ii*) one who has the requisite qualifications, who is fit and capable with body and mind properly tuned.

Mārga means a path, technique or method. There are several paths : the Vaidika, Tāntrika, non-Brāhmanika, as well as the divisions of bhakti, karma, Jñāna, yoga.

In this context the term Bhagavāna refers to one's personal chosen deity. The term Svarūpajñāna refers to the realisation of the true nature of the self. Brahmajñana refers to the realisation of the cosmic process.

Different levels of attainment and different grades of aspirant are mentioned in the scriptures : they are manda, maddhya and tīvra - mild middle and intense in capacity.

In the spiritual pursuit, individual differences of intelligence, capacity, capabilities are recognised. According to the temperament of the aspirant, different paths are recommended :

Bhakti : devotion

Karma : service

Jñāna : knowledge

Yoga : inward discipline

The bhakti and karma paths require unswerving loyalty. These two accept the state of dualism. Bhakti is an attitude, it relies on intense attraction and love for the chosen deity. Service or activity has to be offered.

Karma originally referred to the Vaidika karma including mantra mārga, later, service to humanity came to be included.

Both Jñāna and yoga aim at self realisation, knowing the Cosmic Reality. Normally the path of jñāna refers to Advaita Vedanta and Yoga refers to Aṣtānga yoga of Patanjali. For the Sādhanā of jñāna there is no need for a deity because the quest is for the real Self within. This is the same for yoga also but one of the means of attaining yoga samādhi is Iśwara pranidhāna (ch. 1.23).

In the preliminary stage of sādhanā, the stepping stones are sense control, regulatory practice and moral purity. To build up the character and transform the personality it is necessary to control the senses, to have conviction and to surrender to the chosen ideal. Concentration on the ideal and restraining the mind from its outgoing tendencies are to be practised for directing attention to the psychic centre within.

The structural pattern of sādhanā emphasises the power of will force at every level, whether physical, intellectual or emotional. It is not restrictive in nature. Sādhanā is meant for those who are desirous. The ethical practices are necessary for becoming the perfect medium for the vision.

The term 'yantra' means instrument. In this context it refers to the body, which is the vehicle. The term 'deha' means the body apparatus. The term ādhara means the receptive vehicle. To be fit for the spiritual journey the receptive vehicle has to be properly tuned. The aspirant has to develope discriminatory power (viveka), non-attached feeling for transient objects (vairāgya) and has to avoid self gratification (indriya samyam). The six fold primary qualities are :

Sama-dama : control of mind and control of senses,

Titikṣa : patience, endurance of the opposite (heat-cold),

Uparati : balance in action,

Samādhāna : concentration (manah samyoga), practicing the process of introversion (yogābhyāsa),

Śraddhā : strong conviction and loyalty (niṣthā).

THE METHOD

The Vedic approach (Vaidika karma) is based on elaborate ritual, oblation to fire, chanting mantras and performing sacrifice (yajña). The vedic duties to be performed are nitya karma (every day performance), kāmya karma (occasional performance) and there are also obligatory caste duties to be followed. For instance, after having upanayana (initiation at the thread ceremony) daily observance (sandhyā) has to be performed. According to Manu, Yajñyavalkya and Aśvalāyana, the features comprised of sandhyā are :

Arcanā (worship), Prāṇāyāma (breathing practice), Marjanā (purification), Arghya (offering), Upasthāpanā (sanctifying the body) and Gāyatri (chanting or meditating on the Gāyatrī mantra).

The five daily duties of a householder are : svādhyāya (reading the scriptures), Agnihotra (lighting the fire or oblation), Pitṛtarpaṇa (worship of the ancestors), Bhutāvali (feeding the animals and birds/bhuta. preta. piśācha yajñā), and Atithipujan (hospitality).

The Vidhi (injunction) of Karmakānda (the action portion) are : Yajñā (sacrifice), Dāna (offering gifts), Tapah (austerity) and Kṛya (action) for the fulfilment of desires. The method inspires activity collectively and individually.

The Vedas sing the glory of Ṛta (divine order) Satya (truth), Tapas (penance), Śraddhā (conviction) and Vrata (observance) says S.N. Dasgupta in his History of Indian Philosophy Vol-1 (p. 12).

There was no form or symbol (pratika) in the Vedic sacrificial performance (yajñā), yajñā involves an elaborate form of worship of the Divine nature power. The appropriate deity has to be invoked for each particular sacrifice, whether the aim is seeking wealth, protection, health happiness progeny, awakening the mind or intellect and so on. As the Divinity has no physical appearance, it has to be apprehended through mental and physical perfection, (divya cakṣhu and jñāna) in terms of values culturally obtained. (In ṚK x, 109, 5 we find the expression 'devānām ekam angam', the devas are the same. Also it is mentioned that the divine power is functioning through nature.). In the Āraṇyaka texts, the form of worship mentioned is Upāsanā. This signifies mental worship, alone, thereby avoiding the elaborate external actions with accessories. Texts advocate the giving up of worldly desires and the advice is to become introspective. The method is contemplation on the praṇava mantra Om (the sound symbol of the Divine) and/or prāṇā (the vital air).

The word pratika means symbol, so pratika Upāsanā implies contemplation on some symbolic representation, while Upāsanā literally indicates the mental approach to an ideal ('The Upanisadic Meditation,' 'The Cultural Heritage,' Vol.2) The Bṛhadāraṇyaka, the Kaṭha, the Chāndogya and the Munḍaka give ample evidence of discussion on such

Upāsana. The quest for the knowledge of eternal consciousness within the human psyche had begun. Upāsanā indicates this contemplative discipline. The preparation for such Upāsanā is through śravaṇa (listening) and manana (pondering on the meaning) then nididhyāsana (deep concentration on the heard subject matter) can be reached.

The Purāṇas propāgated for an emotional attitude blended with philosophy and ritual in a more simplified manner. The literature advocates Pratika upāsanā, where the object of adoration, the image/idol (murti) has to be worshipped with feeling and devotion (bhāva-bhakti).

The Vaiṣṇava, Śaiva and Śākta upāsanās are all based on the worship, God with form (Pratika). The bhaktimārga prescribes recitation, glorification, repetition of the name of the deity, archanā (worship with accessories), ārati (showing light), contemplation etc. The path of devotion needs an object to adorn and glorify, to receive an offering of emotion and to surrender to.

The concept of bhagavān with six great qualities grew after the counter movement of Buddhism which had a tremendous influence for many centuries. The Brāhmanical tradition revived again in the 1st century B.C., with a second revival in the fourth century A.D. during the reign of the imperial Guptas. In this phase of development, iconography flourished and ritual worship of the deity became the norm. Mūrti/Pratimā is the visual stimulus, the image of a particular deva (god) or devi (goddess) to rouse emotion. Establishing an attachment and relationship is the aim. Generally the following are the main accessories and items of the puja ritual:

Āsana (seat), svāgatam (welcoming), pādyam (water offering), arghyam (a gift), acamaniyam (water to wash), madhuparkam (a special drink), snānam (bathing), vasanam (clothing), ābharanam (ornaments), sugandham (perfume), dhūpa (incense), dīpa (lamp), naivedyam (food, fruit), mālā (garland), anulepanam (anoenting), namāskāra (bowing/ saluation) and pūjā (chanting, contemplation of the image, offering all items mentioned with appropriate light/lamp, flower, burning incense and champher) anjali (the priest and participants together offer flower), nivedana (surrender mentally/prayer), praṇāma (bowing) with uttering appropriate mantra. In special occasion homa (fire oblation) is also included.

More or less this is the ritualistic procedure followed with some regional variations, the aim is to elicit divine emotion. It is believed that the sincere and methodical performance of such activities generate emotion and reverence. Reason, enquiry, wisdom are not primary for such upāsanā. Bhakti sādhanā teaches the aspirant/seeker to consciously keep the ideal always in mind.

There is no doubt that the solemn execution of these practices with sincerity and faith exerts a great influence on the mind of the performer and the other participants. Thus Worship combines certain physical activities with emotion and rational conviction. This kind of practice is oriented towards habit forming action. It prescribes necessary conducive behaviour and dietary restrications also. The latter being particularly emphasised in Vaiṣnava tradition.

Through worship, study and prayer a taste for higher knowledge develops and self analysis commences. The human mind is always in conflict with the attractions of the outside world, by contemplating the various sports of the Lord the mind gets purified, so that gradually the outgoing tendency is checked and it is prepared to surrender. These are the general concepts and methodology of the devotional path.

A kind of synthetic outlook is observable in the Gita : elements of the Vedic, Upaniṣadic, Yogic and Paurānic concepts are combined. It speaks emphatically to renounce the fruit of karma, though not karma itself : 'karma phala sannyāsa' is the dictum (2.47). Also it is explained in the last chapter that yajña-dāna-tapah-kṛya (sacrifice-gift offering-austerity-work) should not be given up, because karma purifies, it is the fruit of karma that has to be surrender. In other words, there should not be any attachment to or hankering for the result.

The instruction is to develop divine qualities, the twenty six sāttvika gunas are : abhayam (fearlessness), sattvasanśuddhi (pure in heart), dānam (gift offering/alms giving), dama (calmness/restraint), yajñā (performance of sacrifies), svādhyāya (study of the scriptures), tapah (penance), ārjavam (honesty), ahiṃsā (non-injury), satyam (truthfulness), akrodha (free of anger), tyāgah (renunciation), śantih (peace), apaiśunam (non-slander), bhuteṣu dayā (compassion), alolupattam (non-greed), mārdavam (gentleness), hṛh (modesty), acāpalam (non-fickleness), tejah (strength and patience), kṣhamā (forgiveness) dhṛtih (enduring), śaucham (cleanliness), adrohah (non-envy), and nātimānita (non-boasting). These constitute divine wealth, passion for such qualities leads man to the highest goal. The purport is the transformation of personality. In this context it may be explained that aspiration for acquiring such qualities results in gradual progress towards perfection. So characteristically a sāttvika personality possesses divine wealth.

Except for ascetics and students celibacy is not prescribed either in the Vedic practice or on the devotional path.

Sadācāra

This is the guideline for daily practice :

> **prātah smaranam soucam ca snānam cāghamarsanam/ sandhyā japastaparnam ca agnihotram tathārcanam/ mounam dhyānam bhojanam ca sadācārāh prakirtitāh//**

Morning prayer, cleanliness, bathing, expiatory activities, repetition of the Lord's name, or a mantra, offering of water and offering an oblation to the fire, observing silence, doing meditation and eating food in the proper manner are known as Sadācāra (conducive activity).

(Sadācāra of Adi Sankara, commentary by Sudhansu Caitanya, Central Chinmaya Mission Trust Publication, 1988, pp. 13).

The Gita explains three kinds of penance (tapah) and two types of cleanliness (śauca) :

Tapah

(*i*) **Śarīram Tapah :** (Penance of the body)

> **deva-dvija-guru-prājña pujanam śaucam arjavam/ brahmacaryam ahimā ca śarīram tapa ucyate//**

Due (reverence of Gods and Brahmanas, teachers and wisemen, purity, uprightness, chastity, refusal to do harm, (this) is (true) penance of the body).

(*ii*) **Vāṇmaym Tapah :** (Penance of the speech)

> **anudvegakarm vākyam satyam priyahitam ca yat/ svādhyāyābhyāsanam caiva vāṇmayam tapa ucyate//**

Words that do not cause disquiet, [that are] truthful kind and pleasing [as well as] the constant practice of sacred recitation, (this) is the penance of the tongue).

(*iii*) Mānasam Tapah :

manah prasādah saumyatvam mounam ātmavinigraha/
bhāva samśuddhirityetat tapa mānasam ucyate//

Serenity of mind and friendliness, silence and self restraint and the cleansing of one's affections - this is called the penance of the mind.

Śaucam

(*i*) Vāhya śauca (outer cleanliness) cleanliness of the body with water soil etc.

(*ii*) Ābhyantra śauca (cleansing the mind, inward purity) removing attachment and other impurity from the mind and intellect.

(The above translations are taken form Prof. R.C. Zaehner's commentary, The Bhagvad - Gita, pp 378, with slight alteration.)

The paths of devotion and work require unswerving loyalty and love because these are based in duality. These paths are recommended for householders, benevolent service donars and commoners.

For the Sādhanā (discipline) of jñāna (knowledge) there is no need for a deity because the quest is for the real Self within, which we have mentioned already. This is a difficult path. But in all these paths the preliminary stepping stone is control (samjama), regulation (niyama) and regular practice (abhyāsa). Where there is knowledge there is non-attachment (vairāgya) that is, the growing sense of neutrality, impersonal feeling, no show or extravagance and non-enjoyment of luxury. The higher stage of devotion and karma leads to knowledge.

The Devotional path provides instructions for developing intense feeling. According to temperament, the devotee can progress in a natural manner. Through prayers to satisfy one's wants, needs and desires, through effort to be in touch with the divine power, entering into an emotional attachment with all sincerity, the devotee (the person) will eventually attain the delightful experience of pure devotion.

The structural pattern of Śādhanā shows that it is necessary to be disciplined at very level of physical, intellectual and emotional growth. Wholeness develops as the higher consciousness progresses through feeling, intuition, contemplation and meditation. Initiation is an important event in every system.

The ultimate goal of bhakti are Sājujya, Sāmipya, Sālokya-coming nearer to the Lord and being attached to His eternal servitude, as reflected in the famous utterance of Śri Caitanya :

mama janmani janmaniśvare/
bhava tad bhaktirahaituki tvayi//

I desire to serve the Lord with all my heart without a slightest thing to self seeking attitude, birth after birth.

Traditions including the Vaiṣṇava, Śaiva and Śakta emphasise Divine grace : when the Sādhaka successfully accomplishes the preliminary steps, Divine grace (prasāda, kṛpā, anugraha) descends (dawns) upon him. It is considered to be the essential precondition for self realisation, as is the grace of the guru.

YOGA

The term yoga means application of the process of introversion. It is a discipline of body-mind integration, psycho-physical therapy and self-analysis. In conjunction with action and devotion, yoga is accepted by all schools. Although the term yoga has different meanings in different texts.

Yoga emphasises the use of will power : controlling the mental waves through a process of physical and breathing regulation, its primary objective is psychological, leading to one pointed concentration which leads to samādhi.

Broadly speaking the karma and jñāna divisions groups the disciplines as follows : (Hindu Sadhna, Nalinikanta Brahma, p. 67).

KARMA

Karma includes the sacrificial rituals, upāsanā, bhakti, yoga, the Vaiṣṇava, Tantra and Paśupata system of faiths.

Jñāna

Generally the disciplines of philosophical abstraction includes Sāṁkhya and Vedānta, together with Buddhism.

Sankara's Vedāntic interpretation of superimposition (vivarta/adhyāsa), the monastic order (tyāgadharma) and his non-dualistic theory were not accepted by all vedāntists. This resulted in the systems of Viśiṣtādvaita dvaita, Dvaita, Suddhādvaita, Dvaitadvaita and Acintiyabhedābheda etc. The term dvaita is derived from the base 'dvi', the prefix 'a' in the term advaita indicates negation, so this Sanskrit term literally means 'not two'.

The four topics of Vedanta are :

Adhikāri (qualified seeker)

Viṣaya (the subject matter)

Sambandha (the relation : identity)

Prayojana (the purpose).

These are known as anuvandha catuṣṭaya these are the first steps in spiritual practice. The seeker who is aware of the meaninglessness and futility of selfseeking worldly activities will gain from the Vedāntic path. He is qualified who has disciplined his life and developed intense inquisitiveness for self knowledge.

In Advaita exposition Brahman is nirguṇa (attributeless). (the ominscient omnipresent Supreme Being. In other systems Brahman is the repository of all qualities (saguna).

The theory of Advaita accepts the fundamental identity of the individual soul with Brahman. And the interpretation is, that Brahman is not an idea. Brahman is the cause and the effect, in other words the material and efficient cause of the universe, so the relationship of the world and Brahman is non-different (ananya). The ātman (soul) and brahman are one, the existent world is experienced due to the spell of Māyā, i.e., avidyā (ignorance). The soul is eternal and all pervanding (vibhu). Brahman is indefinable (anirdeśya), the absolute Reality. Māyā is a reflection. Advaita Vedānta relates man to the Absolute Reality.

There is only one soul. The duality (multiplicity) we experience is due to agency : different agents mean a different experience. And the sense of duality is due to sensory apprehension. The ātman is encompassed in a body-mind frame. In a time-frame (life span) it appears as if the sense organs and the neural processes produce consciousness (that is, human consciousness). But without the 'Self' there is no consciousness or experience.

A tentative framework is given as follows :

Agency - external objects
↓
Body sense
↓
Inward faculty
↓
Strikes the inteligence
↓
Reasoning faculty → Judgement/knowledge
↓
Abstracting thoughts, experience, image
↓
Unchangeable consciousness *i.e.*, Awareness only = Self.

This Self is the permanent cogniser that witnesses all personal experiences and tendencies. This Self is consciousness itself. Brahman is the ever existing Reality. It is not thought : it is beyond the body and mind (nirviśeṣ cinmātrā).

In spiritual discipline, the two levels of *Vyavahārika* (every day life) and *Pāramarthika* (the spiritual plane/level) are explained as follows :

The *Vyavahārika* is the space-bound, time-limited level of empirical life and events, whereas the *Pāramārthika* should be understood as the higher plane of eternal existence unbounded by time and space.

Avidyā, the natural tendency of mind and body, can be controlled if the functioning of the mind and body's reactions are properly understood.

This objective world of our experience is finite and of man's making; we think in bounded limited logical terms.

Our conscious thought and discursive knowledge cannot fathom or reach the vast infinite eternal Reality. Form the logical point of view, our empirical self and personal experience are our (apparent) reality. The universal consciousness (wholeness) can only be intuitively felt. It is an illuminating experience beyond knowledge.

According to Indian psychology the *inner instrument (antahkaraṇa)* includes the mind, intelligence, ego, and citta (the storing faculty).

Mind (mānas) is the collecting faculty; it receives impressions. *Intelligence (buddhi)* is the decisive faculty which makes decisions. *The Ego (ahamkāra)* is the asserting faculty; *Citta*, the storing faculty, restores.

In the previous section brief mention has been made regarding the functioning of mind, the structure of the organic body, the mechanism of perception (cognition) and inherent impulses (emotion).

The Yoga philosophy admits that the inherent desire for freedom sits side by side with the desire for life and enjoyment, because 'the body is the seat of enjoyment *(bhogāyatana)*'.

The psychology explains that it is the natural tendency of mind to be deluded (identified) with empirical existence, as perception occurs on coming into contact with existing objects.

In the previous section, we have touched upon the cognitive aspect only. In fact, there are three functions of mind : cognitive, emotional and volitional. These three need to be integrated in spiritual practice. When the restless thoughts are gathered together the mind becomes concentrated and relaxation *ensues.* Manas is an internal organ *(jñānendriya)* it can act with past, present and future.

The second aspect of the mind is Emotional modification *(bhāvātmaka).* It includes the emotion of self love *(abhimāna)*, the *tendencies* of attachment *(rāga)*, hatred *(dveṣa)*, jealousy *(hingsā)*, distress *(kleśa)*, egoism *(asmitā)*, desire or will *(icchā)*, and feeling *(anubhava).*

The third aspect is Volitional modifications *(prayajanātmaka),* it covers :

(*i*) *pravṛtti* - inclination for action,

(*ii*) *nivṛtti* - inclination for withdrawal.,

(*iii*) *jivan yoni* - life sustaining spontaneous volition.

The cognitive, emotional and volitional aspects are integrated in the mind's function. Thought, emotion, will, cognition and so on cannot be separated into particular nerve reactions.

Individual

So far, we have described the body mind complex, the working of the mind *(antahkaraṇa)*, and the stratification of the organic and subtle aspects of the body-mind frame. And we have understood that individuality is identified with (centred on) or infused with asmita, which is defined as wrong identifiction of oneself with the body and mind.

A name, a form, an appearance in a time frame, in a situation with cirumstantial limit, some experiences, a bundle of memories- these are the adjuncts of individuality. All these elements surrounding a body-mind complex create a 'vyakti'; in other words these are the construct of and individual.

The aim of 'sādhanā' is to eradicate wrong ideas by means of strong willforce. Intellectual and rational pursuit will check the tendencies of the mind, by developing a deep attachment to an ideal, be it God/deva/devi pratimā or pratika (image). Desire for worldly objects, possessions and wealth can be restricted, by regulating food habits, and by practising physical-external discipline, good health can be maintained. All these are necessary requirements to intensify the desire to experience the real nature of 'I'.

The discipline of yoga asserts that for complete transformation of an individual's nature it is necessary to eradicate past *samaskāras.* Even spiritual testimony does not lead one to that transformation; it only reminds us, it cannot compel us to do so. The persuasion should come from within. So both the external (moral, ethical) and internal (contemplative meditation-based) disciplines are absolutely necessary.

The term 'svarūpa' implies the nature of the self. '*Sva*' means self (own), '*rūpa*' means form, shape. In this context it means 'real nature'. There is a difference between the psychological self 'me' the empirical ego-and the *Puruṣa* 'I', the *ātman* which is *sat-cit-ānanda* (existence-consciousness-bliss), which is *aja-anādi-anata* (unborn-eternal-unending). The seeker has to make use of his faculties and sharpen the instruments to experience the subject who resides within his bodily existence. Having that experience is far form an ordinary sensory perception, it is the '*turīya avasthā*', being steady in consciousness, the highest state of mind.

In Śankara's term this condition is '*aparokṣha anubhuti*' (direct perception), its nature is '*anirvacanīya*' that is, - 'this experience is unexpressible in words'. This term is also used in the Vaiṣṇava philosophy to describe the nature of *bhakti* (devotion): '*anirvacanīya prema svarūpa*'. The mystical state in yoga is the yogic intuition, absorption in one thought-*samādhi.*

The method, the gradual steps towards unification of the mental forces have been mentioned in the previous section. Different types of samādhi are recognised. There are different types of yoga also, each emphasising a different aspect and aiming at different goals. They include :

Haṭha Yoga

Body and breath control. The aim is kāyāsampat (*rūpa* : *beauty*, *lāvanya* : *grace*, *vala* : *strength*). Gaining beauty, grace and strength to avert aging. Disciplining the breath has an influence on the mind. (Ref P.S iii. 45)

Karma Yoga

Selfless Service : perfection (knowledge) through action (*karmasu kausalam* : yogah) (Gita 2.50).

Kṛiya Yoga

Austerity (*tapas*), study (*svādhyāya*), devotion to god (*īśvara pranidhāna*)

Bhakti Yoga

Attaining perfection through devotion; complete surrender to God.

Jñāna Yoga

Attaining wisdom (*prajñā*), '*sthitaprājña*' (Gita 2.55).

Raja Yoga

Training of the mind; withdrawal of the mind form the senses. As the nature of the mind is to flow outwords in the form of vṛtti, control of the ever-flowing current of mental modes (*vṛtti*) to one thought (one object = one pointed) by continuous(conscious) effort is the aim. When the mind turns within and the flow is uninterrupted, it is in the state of meditation (*dhyānāvasthā*).

The mind is material; it is the product of prakṛti. It is not dissolved as long as the material gross body (*jiva-deha*) remains in its normal state of existence. So it is necessary to control distraction (*vikhepa*) by practising dispassion (*vairāgya*). Once 'kaṣāya' (bitterness) is restrained, the favourable condition for concentration will arise. When the mind goes beyond the dualities of *rāga-dveṣa* (attachment and anger), equanimity in the face of pleasure and pain (*sukha-dukha*) prevails.

In absorption (*samādhi*) the identity is felt (*anubhuta*) with the true original nature of the microcosm; it is *amurata*-part and parcel of the universe. The whole universe is the manifestation of brahman. The consciousness within and conscious cosmic energy are but one and the same. The mind is lost in ecstasy. This felt experience and other observed experiences are not the same. When the intuitive insight removes all confusion, no mental mode arises and the yogi is ever-blissful in Kaivalya (Ref. P.S. iii. 54/iv. 34).

It is beyond the power of human language to give an accurate description of such an experience of blissful ecstasy says the Pātañjala Yogasūtra.

The mystical state in yoga is that of yogic intuition, which surpasses the limitations of sensory knowledge.

'amurta' - infinite, 'prapanca' - the manifested diversity, nama rupa, 'murta' - form, a shape, manifestation.

The Yoga Physiology

Scholars are of the opinion that yoga was practised a long time before Patanjali (S. Dasgupta, Yoga as Philosophy and Religion, Preface). The physical body is the vehicle for the expression of inner achievement. The yoga practice involves both external and internal disciplines for fully restraining the citta vṛtti (mental states). Perhaps at a much later time the system of yoga Physiology developed other ideas. Thus comes into it :

(*i*) 700 million naṛis, psychic centres, hidden energy at the base of spine etc.;

(*ii*) ***The Upper Portion :*** The head, trunk, limbs; the lower portion the legs, feet;

(*iii*) ***The Centre*** : The cerebro (spinal column) which supports and controls the whole body;

(*iv*) The brain and spinal cords in the skull. The spinal column is the great centre known as *brahmadanḍa*' (*merudanḍa*). Within this danḍa are the eṛā pingalā and suṣumnā naṛiṣ.

(*v*) ***There are seven (six) plexuses (cakra = circle) :*** *The mulādhāra* (root, support) at the base of the column, and then moving upwards, the *svādhisṭhāna*, *manipura*, *anāhata*, *viśuddha*, *ājñā* and *sahasrāra* cakras.

A description of this nature is not actually found in Pātanjala Yogasutra. However, to grasp the purport of Patanjali's teaching, an integrated study of yoga, philosophy, psychology, cosmology, ethics and religion is necessary.

In Pātanjala Yogasūtra I have Found : Nāvi cakra ('naval circle'), kauṭhakupa ('the pit of the throat'), kūrmanāṛi ('tortoise tube'), murdhā (within the skull), hṛdaya (the heart) and the udāna, prāṇa, samāna, apāna, vyāna (the air = the breathing force) in chapter iii. 28-38 sloka.

According to Prof. S. Dasgupta, the yoga method dates form the time of the Buddha. The idea of self concentration (yoga = absorption) can be traced in the Śvetaśvatara and Kaṭha Upanisads, while in the Maitrāyani the method is in a more developed form. He assumes that a modified form, which was assimilated into the Vedānta, Tantra and Śaiva traditions developed later. He has given some direction of differences citing the Kitab Patanjal of Alberuni. (A History of Indian Philosophy, Vol. 1 pp. 227, 235).

Vedānta is the climax of Vedic wisdom. It removes ignorance by subjugating the forces of nature externally and within; it enhances the inherent capacity of man, establishing him in his pristine glory realisation of his real (sva) rūpa, the *ātmạn*. The *ātman* is neither matter nor mind but the ground of both the physical and mental states of existence. Consciousness is the basis of all psychic and physical experiences. The mind is limited in time and space, while consciousness is unlimited. The mind is sensation and brain; it is an instrument; it can undertake a series of activities, through which knowledge can arise. Continuity of individual awareness is possible for consciousness, for it is nothing but part and parcel of cosmic energy, which is conscious and ever-present-the absolute infinite *brahman*. The cosmos is the expression, the manifestation of 'That'. Therefore, the seeker should have a proper understanding of the following :

1. The relationship between the body and the world, between the mind and body and between pure consciousness and mind.
2. ***The Ordinary World*** : The world of objects (*jaṛa padārtha*) is experienced in each given situation or body.
3. The object is experienced by a subject; the body is the medium/means/instrument - the subject is 'I'.

4. ***Mental Status*** : *Vṛtti*, *antahkaraṇa* - are the states of cognition, feeling and will. At the time of perception 'the mental and the physical coalesce'.
5. Mental perception (*mānasa pratyakṣa/ anuvyvasāya*) when things of the world are reexperienced through :
   (*a*) psychological introspection (non-cognitive feeling, will),
   (*b*) reflective introspection/ spiritual introspection, - that is the Sāksī (witness).
6. Psychological introspection is dependent, while the spiritual introspection is self-revealing-subjectivity itself (*avacchedabhāva*).

This transcendental state occurs on withdrawal form the surroundings. At the ideal stage of perfection there is no point of reference. *Nāma rūpa* (name and form) is but the symbolice representation. But withdrawal alone is not the final realisation. It is Direct awareness-*i.e.*, the experience of subjectivity (which is reflective and dissociative) — of the impersonal Consciousness.

This may give rise to the logical argument that as long as the seeker remains as an individual person he has a concrete living experience and an individual subjectivity-how then can he pass on to impersonal Consciousness?

The methodology given is that this logical argument has a very insignificant place in *advaitavāda*. The aspirant needs to rely on the living experiences which are recorded in the scripture and which are explained and taught by the realised Guru (A Modern Understanding of Advaita Vedanta, Prof. Kalidas Bhattacharya, pp. 50-51).

Following the instructions; purify the mind by developing *viveka*, *vairāgya*, *śamatā* and *mumukṣuttva*;

understand the purport of the Upaniṣads through *śravaṇa*, *manana* and *nididhyāsana* then apply the yoga process of concentration and meditation and realise the truth *i.e.*, cognitively discover or arrive at impersonal pure Consciousness.

The ultimate principle is perceived; it is knowledge itself-*jñānam* dawns upon the seeker. What is the end result? Feeling identity, it is self illumination, transformed his personality.

śānta mahānta nivasanti santa/
vasantavat lokahitam caranta//

'Realised souls are calm and benevolent; they live like the spring air sharing their hearts' bounty with all humanity.

tīrnāh svayam bhīmabhavārṇava janā/
nahetunā nyānapi tārayantah//

(*Vivekacūṛāmani of Sri Śamkaracarya, sloka*-37)

'As they have transcended the misery of life (samsāra) they spread their knowledge unasked, to help other to cross'.

However, self effort is the main thrust in Advaita Vedānta.

Other Vedantic methods of enquiry differ. The line of thought found in the Bṛhadāranyaka (iv.3.21), Taittiriya (ii.7), and Chāndogya (iv.10.4) Upanisads rests on bliss, happiness and all absorbing love : a delightful rapture which is not really like the macro cosmic and micro cosmic identity. In these texts Self-realisation (God-realisation) is dependant on the Lord's favour.

The other Vadanta system emphasises bhakti (devotion). Mention has been made regarding puja, upāsana and contemplative yoga efforts, as well as listening to God's name (Hari kathā prasanga), japa (repeating the holy name), singing his glory, bowing to the *Vigraha* (image), prayer, remembrance, giving service and self dedication and directing all thoughts to God. *Prapatti or śaranāgati* (surrender) is here the main pathway to God-realisation, because only with His grace (kṛpā) does realisation descend upon the devotee. The gist of the teaching is complete self surrender and constant remembrance of God (*sadānurakti*).

Of course self effort and will force are primary for a spiritual aspirant and to make any progress in spiritual path the mind has to be tamed :

mano nāma mahā vyāghra viṣayāranyabhumiṣu caratatra...............//

"In the forest [tract] of sense pleasures there prowls a huge tiger called the mind....." (Vivekacūṛāmani, sloka - 176, Tr. by Swami Mādhavānanda).

Again the precept is that the mind is to be utilised to engage in the inward-looking process.

manah pramādah puruṣasya bandho/
manah prasādo bhavabandha mukti//

(*Sarva Vedānta Siddhant Sangraha sloka*-374)

'The disturbed mind is the cause of bondage, whereas tranquility leads to [brings home] salvation'.

'Three immortal precepts (footsteps).......when practised lead to heaven - selfrestraint, charity and conscientiousness'.

trini amruta-padāni-(su) anuṭhitāni
navamti svaga dama chāga apramāda/

(From the Brahmi inscription on Besnagar column, printed in Cultural Heritage, Vol. 2).

As *pratipaksha bhāvanā* (counter thought) is a useful method in yoga to tame adverse thoughts so also the *satsanga* is an important opportunity to develop the correct mental attitude for bhakti :

Satsangatve nihsangatva nihsangatve parma tattva//

'In keeping company with the wise one can develop a detached attitude (to worldly objects). In the state of detachment, higher thoughts arise.'

And 'when the sense of ego subsides, the ideal sprouts, the glow shines' :

ahama hantaya sphurati parama tattva/

Parājñā, the knowledge (Reality) descends when the ego is annihilated.

So far we have outlined the Vaidika - Pourānika methodology; now we turn to the Tāntrika method. There are several *āmnaya* (schools), *ācāras* (paths), *matas* (views) and *sampradāyas* (sects) in the Tantra tradition. There are three main division based on regional differences the Viṣṇukrāntā from the Vindhya Hills to Jāvā, the Rathakrānta form the northern side of Java to Mahacina and the Asvakrānta - the country westward. It is said that - each of these regions has 64 Tantras.

Again there are four sampradāyas (traditions Sects) : the Gauṛa in the East, the Kerala in the Middle, the Kāshmira in the West and the Vilāsa, which is found in all regions.

According to Tantra, three kinds of dispositions are prominent in human beings. They can be classified as divya (divine), Vira (heroic) and Paśu (animal). According to his natural disposition, each person views things differently for everyone is endowed with different qualities. Therefore, the rules of conduct will vary. There are seven ācāras : Veda, Vaiṣṇava, Śaiva, Dakshina, Vāma, Siddhānta and Kaula. It is said the first three are meant for Paśubhāva, the next two suit the Virabhāva, and the last two are for the advanced (divyabhāva). In other words the gradual ascendence are indicated : an aspirant following śauca, bhakti, jñāna, then consolidating what has been achieved can attain bhoga (enjoyment for one's own sake), then can renounce, the final stage is the Kaula, which is dependant on the cosolidation of the merits and demerits of all.

Initiation is vital in this tradition. An aspirant is initiated by the Guru (a realised person). According to the type and capacity of the aspirant as judged by the Guru he is given the mantra and instruction follows.

The *praṇava mantra* (OM) is very important in all traditions. The three sounds, and their representation by the three letters a, u and m, are explained in various ways :

(*i*) as characterising the three gunas (sattva, rajas and tamas); as the subtle form of the sacred formula '*hamsah*' (which means the life breath), and as the 'Trivindu' representing Brahma, Viṣṇu and Maheśvara, where Brahma equals a, Viṣṇu is u and Maheśvara is m, Three forming the word form of śabda-brahma, sound symbol of the Absolute;

(*ii*) as combination of Aham and Idam, combination of icchā, jñāna, kṛyā;

(*iii*) the nasal sound is represented by (m). The curve is explained as Kalā and the dot within as nāda-vindu. It is further explained as *nirguṇa brahma mahākāla*, that is Sadāśiva is the vindu. And the kalā-vindu combination is *prakṛti* which is the *kulakundalni* Śakti lying dormant in all living beings.

Lord Brahma is the creative aspect and hamsah is the vāhana (vehicle) of Brahma.

The *Omkara* is an *ajapa mantra*-uncreated sound. Śiva is the formless Absolute, when dissociated form Prakṛti (śakti) Śiva with form (saguṇa) emanates tattva (substance), desire (vicikirshā) as vindu and bursths forth into nāda. *Nāda* is *Śabda-brahma*; thought (language) ensues. All creation is the manifestation of the *nāda* vibration.

In the Tantra tradition, the letters of the alphabet are known as mātṛka. Audible sound passes through several levels. The lowest or base level in the *mulādhāra cakra* is just expressed as vibration (parā). Once it takes shape, it enters the stage of '*pasyanti*' the next one is *madhyamā* when it arrives at *anāhata*. The articulated sound is produced by the vocal opparatus in the stage of *vaikhari*. Words are formed with letters, mantras are uttered in sounds. The sounds and letter of alphabet are very important. Mantras give form to the deity and rouse consciousness, so that everything comes within the range of comprehension.

It is generally accepted that there are six cakras. The base is *mulādhāra* (the region of earth, situated at the foot of the spine) where the spiritual energy remains coiled and takes the form of a four petalled lotus. Above this is the *svādhisṭhāna* (the region of water) as a six petalled lotus and just above it at the navel is the *manipura* (the region of fire), a ten petalled lotus. Next is the *anāhata* in the region of the heart (the region of air), containing twelvepetals, and above this is *visuddha* (the region of ākāśa) at the base of the throat, with sixteen petals. Between the two eyebrows is the *ājñā* (the psychic centre) with two petals. On piercing all these, the coiled energy flows upwards to reach the *sahasrāra* in the cerebrum, manifesting its full glory. The chakras are non physical psychic centres implying the levels of consciousness. The dormant energy that is kula (in other words 'Kāli') by means of the 'stress' or effort of willforce a combination of vital air and the fire of desire in the Sādhaka rises. (Tantra Tattva Pravesika, Swami Prajñānānada, pp. 42-3 147).

There are elaborate descriptions of the mātṛikāvarṇas. Dhani (sound) and the symbol of it in language (Sanskrit) is mātrika in Tantra. Various sounds and mantras belong to the varṇamālā (the 50 letters/sound symbols of Sanskrit language). Each of them has been defined in several ways: through colour (varṇa), svarūa, abhirupa, mahimā, kalā, śakti, devatā, ṛṣi and rhythm. A sādhaka has to comprehend the inner meaning and significance of each and imagine that each lotus of the cakra is infused with all these terms. With strong faith, conviction and devotion, the aspirant has to proceed under the able guidance of the realised Guru.

In the discipline of awakening the spiritual energy the first step is purification (śuddhi), the second is 'lifting' and the third is realisation (caitanya), significantly meaning the union of Śiva - Śakti, the transcendental stage. In this condition, complete transformation occurs which is known as 'Śiva-Śakti sāmarasya'. (kula = Kāli, kundalini = in coild from; another name is 'ādhāra śakti = basic energy', said M.M. Gopinath Kaviraja).

Swami Prajnanananda has made a comparison between the cakra mentioned in the Tantra (and later Yoga texts) and the kosa (sheaths) mentioned in Vedanta :

	Cakra	*Kosa*
1.	Mulādhāra	Annamaya
2.	Svādhisṭhāna	Prāṇamaya
3.	Manipura	Manomaya
4.	Anāhta	Manomaya
5.	Viśuddha	Vijñānamaya
6.	Ajñā	Ānandamaya
7.	Sahasrāra	Sattvamaya (Tantre Tattva 0 Sādhana, p. 1471).

Meditation

There are three types :

Sthula : When it is desired to experience the chosen deity or rupa with form and shape.

Jyotirdhyāna : When the object of meditation is the light of consciousness, envisaged in the form of a light.

Sukhsma : When the Vindu-brahma and Kulakundalini śakti is felt.

Just below the ājñā cakra on the twelve-petalled lotus, the effulgent Sri Guru in the form of Hamsa is seated. It must be both felt and seen. Samādhi occurs when the sādhaka's own sense of self dissolves into the all-pervanding effulgent Consiousness.

In Tantra mudrā, haṭhayoga, sodhana and nādānusandhan are very important discipline. Nādānusandhāna refers to how the three naṛis that is, Iṛa, Pinglā and suṣumnā to be used in flowing through cakras, the Base energy to be taken towards the cerebral. Purging refers to the purificatory rites.

Mantra

The Vaidika mantra Gāyatrī and the Tantrika mantra

Mātrikā are 'verṇa mayi' *i.e.*, they are expressed in sound and symbol, with a power beyond comprehension. These mantras are the vehicle of sādhanā. The varṇa creates form (rupa) and thought (bhāvarā). With proper pronunciation and understanding, the meaning of Vija (the seed mantra) is revealed. Meditation on the vija leads to perception of the deity.

Japa

Each sound symbol is the indicator of a particular divine form (devata). Japa is regular repetition of these sound symbols.

Yantra

Yantra is a symbolic diagram of the deity which is worshipped in ritual practice in place of murti as the symbolic representation of the deva or devi. The diagram is different for each deity.

The Śriyantra represents Śrividyā. Yantra is seen as the same as cakra. It is considered to be living, vested with power, mantra and energy. Mantra gives potency to the cakra.

There are 16 petals, nine cakras and four gates in the Śriyantra (or Śricrakra). All the varṇas, vargas and triangles have significant meanings. In the middle is the vindu indicating Śiva-Śakti in an avinābhāva relation 'like a blackgram seed' i.e. it has two parts in one whole from.

Tantra Sādhan (Śakti Sādhanā)

This sādhanā involves following the methods as prescribed in the various Tantra texts. There are 36 tattvas that should be properly understood by the aspirant.

There are three types of texts those spoken by Śiva - the Āgama, those spoken by Śakti, - the Nigama and the Bhairava tradition of Yamala. (P.C. Bagchi in Studies on the Tantra).

Āmnāya Classification

The Lord has five faces; the Āgamas are classified accordingly :

the eastern (sadyajāta) face = Purvāmnaya,

the western (Tatpuruṣa) face = Pascimāmnaya,

the northen (Vāmadeva) face = Uttarāmnaya,

the southen (Aghora) face = Daksināmnaya,

the upper (Iśāna) face = Urdhāmnaya.

The ācāras have already been mentioned. The Kaulacaris are Kaula, i.e., they are worshipper of Kāli. Besides these seven ācāras there is Samyācāra, which is adopted and followed by the South Indian Śrividyā sampradāya (sect). There is not much external ritualistic methodology in this practice. Devi Tripurā (Tripurāsundari) herself is Śrividyā and Ṣoṛaśi, Lalitā. Lalitā is worshipped as Kāli or Daksinakāli in North India. (The 19th century sādhaka Sri Ramakrishna of Bengal did his Tantra sādhanā following this method inspired by his Guru Brāhmanī). The Samyacaṛi mainly practices internal upāsanā (meditation, Kula kundalini jāgaran), the yantra being mentally visualised through the use of mantra. The yantra or Śricakra symbolises 'the universe (both macrocosm and microcosm) and its divine cause.' The method of absorption is prescribed for the sādhaka. (The Cultural Heritage of India, Vol. IV p. 258).

There are three main schools :

Kashmira : Pratyāvijñā - Trika (Spanda) samprādaya.

Gouṛa : Worship of Kali with emphasis on experimental ritual practice.

Kerala : The Śrividyā sect - worship of Śricakra (śriyantra).

According to their chosen deity, sects are classified as either Śaiva or Śākta, though ultimately, they agree that Śiva and Śakti are not different. When Nirguṇa Brahman Śiva desires to create He takes the form of dancing Kāli. The theory of reflection in Kashmiriya Śaiva philosophy views this world (jagat, viśwa prapanca) not as false appearance but as the expression (vikāśa) and reflection of Śiva's power. So the sādhaka undertakes the effort (sādhanā) to realise the 'sāmarasyānubhuti (unity/non-difference) of Śiva and His Śakti. While the conceptual analysis may differ, the ultimate aim is basically the same in all the schools of Tantra, despite the fact that in some sects, the attainment of ācāra siddhi or miraculous power receives more attention.

Ritual worship

In worship, the ritualistic procedure includes nyāsa, mudrā, bhutasuddhi, prānayāma, dhyāna, prānapratisṭhā, mānasa-pujā and bāhya-puja. Through these, the object of worship, the worshipper and the means and action of worship are transform into an intergrated whole. The acions are elaborate and complicated. Finally in the bāhya-pujā there is the homa - the ritualistic fire oblation - denoting submission and complete surrender, begging for divine grace (as I have understood form my observation and study). The word 'nyāsa' refers to the 'assignment of the various parts of the body to different deities'. The word 'bhutasuddhi' means purification of the body with dripping water surrounding the body, imagining that it is safeguarded by flame. Prāṇapratisṭhā' is the ritualistic infusion of life-breath (awakening the deity). Mudrā is the gesture by moving hands and fingers. There are 50 different kinds of mudrā which are used in rituals. Some of them can be observed in different murtis. Tāntrika mudras are 25 in number, some are very difficult and complicated.

Bāhya-pujā is the elaborate external or exterior rituals, where as the mānasa-pujā refers to mental worship with mantra.

The Tattvas

Śaiva-thirty-six, Vaiṣṇava-thirty-two, Sāṁkhya-twenty-four.

In the Tantra sādhanā the aspirant has to learn thirty-six tattvas :

Śiva, Śakti, Sadāśiva, Vidaghana, Māyā, Avidyā, Kāla, Rāga, Kalā, Niyati, Jiva/Puruṣa, Mana, Buddhi, Ahamkāra, Panca-jñānendriya, Pancakarmendriya, Pancatanmātra, Panca-mahābhuta, Prakṛti and Iśvara. Śiva (brahman) is transcendent (nirguṇa). When associated with Śakti, Śiva becomes saguṇa. Śiva the supreme, expressing creative desire (the inherent upādhi of the absolute) become the Śiva tattva. Śakti as the power/energy of Śiva is the Śakti tattva.

Sadāśiva is the whole universe. When he feels its entirety within himself he is Aham, the Self.

When he looks at his creation, that is the feeling of Idam-non-self.

The significance of the Aham, Idam (ahantā-Idantā) principle is explained in this manner. The Māya tattva, the veil, the limiting aspect of unity and difference is the subject matter of the Avidyā tattva.

The ralationship between the Jiva and Śiva covered in the Kalātattva, where the Jiva is evolving with rāga, kāla, avidya and niyati etc. The concepts of Prakṛti, manah, buddhi and ahamkara are all included in every philosophical discussion. As well as these, respective internal-external organs of the body-mind complex and the five natural elements and their subtle forms are analysed.

This in a nuṭshell is the conceptual knowledge an aspirant has to grasp. This is the discipline that leads the sādhaka step by step towards the restoration of his real nature-the essence Śiva-Śakti within (atman).

(See the explanation given by Swami Prajñānanda in Tantre Tattva of Sādhanā, pp. 64-5).

All the paths whether of Karma, Bhakti, Jñāna, Yoga or Tantra are experimental. All the tattvas and theories are purely human concepts, yet are extermely valuable to those who believe in them. The initiated ones understand their significance; to them it is living experience. Language plays an important role in the religious and philosophical literature. Human imagination starts with the known, within the range of experience, and then transcends it. At that point language becomes suggestive and symbolic.

The Reality (in Vedic terms 'the Brahman') is neither male nor female nor neuter. It is (or it may be) the ever existing power/potency/energy/creativity, which is designated in the śāstras as the cosmic Sattā (Being). Brahman is considered to be the all pervading male principle, while the creative aspect is the female principle. The two cannot be separated, they are like fire and its heat.

In Tantra they become Śiva-Śakti. One of the mahāvākyas in the Upanisads declares : 'Tat tvam asi' - the 'tat' indicates That which is all pervading in the cosmos. It is difficult to understand these abstract philosophical concepts. To our mind, the murti (presentation with form) or even the symbolic representation is more comprehensible. So in the puja Lord Śiva with his consort or Mahā Viṣṇu with Mahā-Lakshmi are worshipped either together or independently or even in pratika, such as the *Śivalinga* or *Śālagramaśilā*. For instance the *kumbha* (pitcher) represents the womb and the water in it symbolises the original source of life. Even without knowing the significance, the puja upakaraṇa (the accessories) are organised and used with sincerity and devotion.

We have mentioned the krama (steps) of the pujā ritual followed in the Tantrika method. The Vaidika - Pourānika pujā is also performed in a similar fashion : (*i*) sankalpa (wish/desire) āhabhāna (welcoming), swastivacana (auspicious words), (*ii*) nyāsa or pratisthāpana (purification of the body by mantra and mudrā, positing different devatā on the body, there by divinising it). There are several kinds of nyāsa. (*iii*) bhutaśuddhi - sancitifying the gross body with mantra and dripping water surrounding the body as if it is safeguarded by flame. It is a kind of preliminary psychological preparation for worship. The word 'pancanga śuddhi' means purification of atma, sthana, mantra, deva and dravya.

(*iv*) Remembering the deity to be invoked, the worshipper has to imagine that he is lighting the fire and being surrounded by its flame. Withdrawing form mundane attraction, with devotion he directs his mind to the feet of Parama Śiva through the channel of suṣmnā.

The term 'nyās' literary means 'sparśa' (touch). Elaborate and complicated actions are prescribed for external worship. We have already mentioned some. (*v*) Prāṇa-pratisṭhā, which actually means invoking the deity, breathing life into the idol. It is performed with ritual actions and mantra. The murti is thenceforth considered to be alive. The worshipper, (*vi*) his mind now emotionally saturated, performs the systematic pujā the ritual, which includes both bāhya (external) and mānasa/antra (internal). (*vii*) Finally, the homa (fire oblation) is done. The ritual fire offering is a kind of catharsis, a surrendering of the ego. There are various kind of homa.

(*viii*) Then to be performed ārātrika, puspānjali and praṇāma. The ārātrika or ārati refers to the waving of lights, incense and the use of a conchshell with water in it, fan, flowers, a piece of cloth, burning camphor and so on. The puṣpānjali refers to the offering of flowers taken in both hands, while chanting the mantra. Praṇāma refers to the obeisance made while uttering the mantra.

While there may be some variations between the Vaidika Pourānika and Tāntrika rituals as well as regional variations, the idea seems to be the same. Mantras also differ in these different traditions.

The mental ritual (mānasa pujā) is the opposite of the bāhya pujā. There are no external accessories, only vāk-mana-hṛdaya (speech-mind and the heart). This inner sādhanā involves mantra, concentration, contemplation and meditation.

Gurupādukā

One of the very significant aspect of sādhanā is the Gurupādukā. This term refers to the seat of Śri Guru. Śri Guru is no other than the Parama Śiva (Śiva with Śakti) or (Iṣṭa).

The word 'pādukā' literally means footwear, and the word 'Guru' means teacher, preceptor. But the compound word in the context of sādhnā has a special meaning. Although the human guru is always respected.

The siddha guru's pādukā is venerated, even it may be installed in the sect's āśhrama or Math. But the philosophical term 'Gurupādukā' is significantly referring to the 'pitha' (seat/place) where the Guru to be installed mentally, *i.e.*, the Hamsa (Śri Guru) has to be meditated upon the crown of the head, as the Sahasrāra is the piṭha.

Source of the Tantra Philosophy

Regarding the Tantra philosophy scholars have the opinion that with all its multifarious development the Tantra philosophy is basically an amalgam of Śāmkhya and Advaita. (see M.M. Gopinath Kaviraj, Tantra Āgama Śāstrer Nidarśan, vol. 1, pp. 60 and Sivajivan Bhattacharya's article, Desh, April 16, 1988).

Reciporcally the Hindu pujā system has been greatly influenced by the Tantric custom. In fact the custom of Initiation, which is such an important event in a sādhaka's life is of Tantric origin.

Summary

We summarise the Tantra mode of sādhanā and its philosophy using Sir J.G. Woodraffers words : 'Śiva is the transcendent, Śakti is the immanent aspect of the one Brahman who is Śiva-Śakti'. (Studies on Tantra, p. 127)

Now the conclusion may be derived that Parama Śiva is the underlying consciousness of cosmic creation, the tattvas are explanations of ingredients and Śakti is His creative power ('cosmic energy'). (see S.B. Dasgupta, Aspect of Indian Religious Thoughts, p. 152, Firma KLM, Calcutta 1977).

The spiritual practice (sādhanā) demands physical, mental and intellectual training of an aspirant (sādhaka), as his whole attitude and personality change (modification/transformation) is the aim.

The Vaidika yajñā, Pouranika pujā (devotional/ offerings), Vicāra (philosophical pursuit), Sādhyaya (śāstra pāṭh/scriptural study), Yoga and Tantrika methodology all are beneficial means and ways for spiritual awakening and progress or advancement in spiritual path.

Any means may be attempted according to the temperament and capacity of the seeker (sādhakā). The aspirant (seeker) or even a common person in faith is allowed to grow according to his/her ability and choice. Whichever may be the way, the goal is the same.

It is beautifully expressed in Śivamahimnāh stotra by the composer Puṣpadanta :

> **trayī sāmkhyam yogam paśupatimatam vaiṣna-vamiti/**
> **prabhinne prasthāne paramidamadah pathyamiti ca/**
> **rucinām vaicitryādṛjukuṭilanānā pathajuṣām/**
> **nṛṇāmeko gamyastvamasi payasāmarṇava iva//**

The Upanisads paved the way of pratika upāsanā. The six yogic angas were the basis of mental approach. The suṣ umma is referred to as Indrayoni (Taittiriya, Ist chapter 6th anuvak, i). Later the system of discipline has been elaborated.

However, whether it is external or internal worship, whether the method is Vaidika, Pourānika or Tantrika; whether the aspirant follows bhakti, jñāna, or yoga paths the idea seems to be the same - control of the senses, developing mental attitude, withdrawal form the external object's attraction and concentration. It is believed that such attentive force of mind brings a sādhaka in face to face with Truth (Reality).

The Upaniṣadic instruction is to meditate upon the Self in the region of heart (yo devo nithitam guhāyam/, Taittiriya

2, ii). Tantra teaches that the seat of Parama Śiva is on the crown of the head (sahasrāra). Patanjli yoga sutra gives elaborate instruction of aṣṭanga method. Later the Kundalini jāgarana at several cakras became essential part of the yoga method. And more or less the yoga methodology of introversion is accepted and adopted in practice by most of the sādhan mārgas.

The Upanisadic mantra 'OM' the symbol of Divinity (Māṇḍukya, i Muṇḍaka, ch. 11, 4), three states of consciousness corresponding with the letter - a u m - the waking, dreaming and deepsleep referring to the gross, the subtle and causal world has been explained in several other ways in various disciplines. For example in Tantra it is explained as sṛsṭi, sthiti and pralaya. Besides the philosophical meaning, the three sound and their letter symbols have been attributed with more properties also. (Tantre Tattva O Sadhana, Prajñānānanda, p. 131)

Finally, though traditionally the two lines of development have been mentioned as karma and jñāna, our study gives an impression that karma, jñāna and bhakti are integrated in sādhanā. However, the two lines of development in sādhanā may be marked by the aspect of emphasis; while one emphasises devotion the other puts importance on the experimental methodology.

Role of Language

Language is an intrinsic aspect of human inheritance. All languages are genuinely complex system of sound and meaning. Language is used in ordinary every day life and it is the tool (medium) of expression for thoughts and ideas.

The world of ideas, relationship, name and forms are dependent on language. The experience of the past is recorded in it. The way a community perceives the world is reflected in its language. Human cognition is mostly dependent on language and is expressed in words (śabda).

A word has its literal, suggestive and intended meanings. A common word used in religious philosophical literature indicates different shades of meaning. The language of such text is often suggestive and containing significant purports. For proper understanding of the meaning intended appropriate explanation is needed.

Above all to grasp the spirit of scriptural content some knowledge of the theoretical conceptions seems to be also necessary. For instance Advaitavedānta declares that 'ātyantika dukha mukti' and 'sukha prapti' is the ultimate gain of sādhanā. According to Yoga 'kaivalya prāpti' is the aim. The concept of mukti differs in different tradition, so also the concept of sukha. Again there is no particular yardstick to measure the experience of dukha - unsatisfactory condition, incompleteness, sorrow, grief or frustration and so on. The term 'kaivalya' refers to an experience, a state of mind.

Perhaps considering the complex nature of language and to avoid misconception, one of the instruction is, to follow a path be firm in that particular way or hold on to that methodology and go forward, proceeding to the path of inquiry with devotion and conviction.

Foot Note

Trayi = Veda, Samkhyam = Samkhya philosophy, Yogam = Yoga philosophy, Paśupatamata = Śaiva scriptures, Vaiṣṇavam = Vaiṣṇava scriptures, iti = thus, prabhinne = divided, prasthane = in this philosophical texts, parama = the best, idam = this, atah = that, pathyam = beneficial, iti = thus, ca = and/ ṛju = straight/ easy, kuṭila = curved, nṛnām = men, eko = one, gamya = goal/ target, tvam = you, asi = are, payasam = rivers arṇava = sea, iva = as/the like. rucinām = tastes/temperament, viacitryat : differences exist.

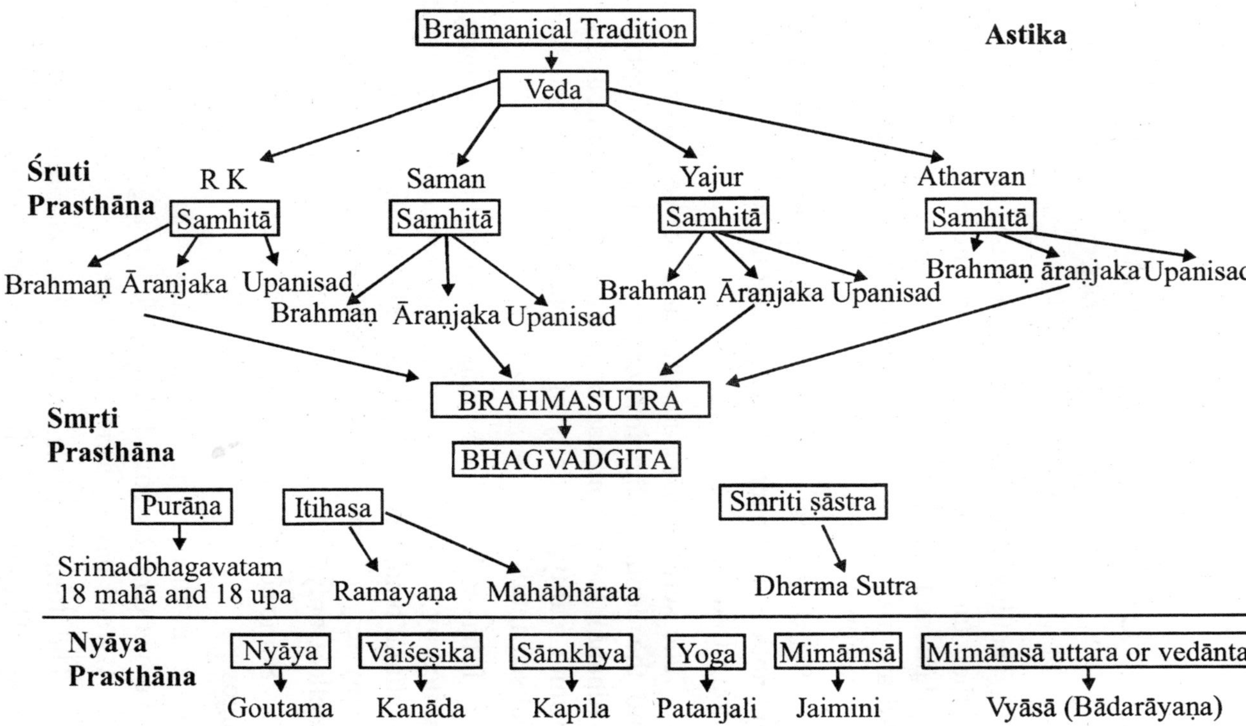

Astika
Brahmanical Tradition
Veda
Śruti Prasthāna
R K
Samhitā
Brahmaṇ Āraṇjaka Upanisad
Saman
Samhitā
Brahmaṇ Āraṇjaka Upanisad
Yajur
Samhitā
Brahmaṇ Āraṇjaka Upanisad
Atharvan
Samhitā
Brahmaṇ āraṇjaka Upanisad
BRAHMASUTRA
BHAGVADGITA
Smṛti Prasthāna
Purāṇa
Srimadbhagavatam
18 mahā and 18 upa
Itihasa
Ramayaṇa
Mahābhārata
Smriti ṣāstra
Dharma Sutra
Nyāya Prasthāna
Nyāya
Goutama
Vaiśeṣika
Kanāda
Sāmkhya
Kapila
Yoga
Patanjali
Mimāmsā
Jaimini
Mimāmsā uttara or vedānta
Vyāsā (Bādarāyaṇa)

LANGUAGE, WORDS AND CONCEPTS

The linguistic forms and expressions are very important as they unfold ideas, they contain the core value system, fundamental thoughts, attitudes, concepts of a community and are used as the medium of communication. Sanskrit is no exception.

Sanskrit language has a long tradition, the concepts and notions had been developed and treated in the course of a long tradition.

The scriptures assure that in case we aspire to delve into the depth of the mystery by making constant effort (sādhanā), the bottom can be reached. The cosmic span, the infinite reality, the unity of the phenomenal world may be realised intuitively.

It has to be borne in mind also that human language is limited by its worldly meaning, and scriptural language has a cultural boundary. Religion and philosophy indicate a glims of mystery of the beyond which can not be fathomed by intellect only.

Some concepts and words are collected in the following pages :

Sanskrit equivalent for the term word is 'śabda'. Śabda is a cover term for sound, linguistic form, grammatical form etc. A word has its form and content.

The form indicates a unit, *i.e.*, combination of oral sounds. The content refers to the meaning of a form.

ओम=प्रणव मन्त्र, Symbol of divinity, epithet of viṣṇu = eternal Being

Praśña Upanisad explains :

अ = earthly existence, phenomenal world, human waking state (मनुष्य लोक)

उ = divine existence, dream state (देव लोक)

म = eternal existence, bliss state (ब्रह्म लोक)

The Sacred syllabus containing three sounds is considered to be representing three Gods :

अ = Visnu,

उ = Śiva

म = Brahmā

From the point of view of linguistics OM can be analysed as follows :

अ The beginning, उ The upper level or middle and म the end or final sound that can be produced through the mouth cavity of human beings, in other words it is referring to the range of speech sound.

मन्त्र = a praise, a scared prayer, hymn, a verse, that elevates the mind, by uttering those sound combinations the mind gets purified.

प्रणव = Om sound, Śabda

श्रुति = hearing, the Veda, sacred knowledge received through listening, hearing.

The knowledge dawns upon, reflected in the heart of the ṚSIS. The mantras uttered spontaneously.

श्रौत = Veda vihita *i.e.*, prescribed by the Veda.

श्रोत्रिय = proficient in Vedic knowledge, well versed in the Veda, a class of brahmin, a learned brahmin.

श्लोकः = a hymn, a verse of praise or a stanza in Anushṭubha metre

स्तुति = song of praise, eulogy, laudation

स्तवः = verses of praise (most cases longer verses for recitation), eulogium, ode

स्मृति = memory, remembering the experience or knowledge gathered before, recollection

स्मृति(शास्त्र) = traditional law, that was delivered by human authors, the body of remembered literature (sacred tradition) including sutra, Dharma Śāstra, purāṇa and Itihāsa.

स्मार्त = one who follows the traditional law, a brahmin well versed in Smṛti.

न्यायः = logic, code of low, a system of philosophy, method of reasoning

नैयायिकः = a logician, one who follows the Nyāya system of philosophy

प्रस्थान = departure, a course to attain, method, a way

श्रुति प्रस्थान = following the path of Vedic dictates

स्मृति प्रस्थान = following the path of traditional way

न्याय प्रस्थान = reasoned method, the conclusion derived after reasoning, following the system of philosophy

प्रस्थान त्रय = the three steps, three ways

प्रस्थान त्रयी = Upaniṣad, Gita, Brahmasūtra

यज्ञः = offering, sacrificial rite, 'Setting up of the sacrificial fire' (agniādhāna)

याज्ञिक = a ritualist, a priest performing a sacrifice (ritual)

हविः = oblation : with milk, clasified butter, Porridge and Cake

अग्निहोत्र = daily offering of milk to the fire in the morning and evening

दर्शपूर्णमास = new and fullmoon sacrifies

ब्रह्मयज्ञः = Vedic recitation

देवयज्ञः = offering to the Gods with melted butter in fire = homa

पितृयज्ञः = an obdation to the Manes

मनुष्ययज्ञः = hospitality to the Brahman mendicants

आश्रमधर्म = the duties of four stages of life

पुरूषार्थ = the four objects of human pursuit, aims of existence

अधिकारभेदः = differentiation in capacity, distinctive authority, the right of performing religious rites.

कर्मफलवाद = the theory of consequence resulting form acts of precious birth, fruit of actions done in a former life.

अतिन्द्रिय = beyond the senses

अतीन्द्रियज्ञान = trancendental knowledge.

ब्रह्मज्ञान = spiritual knowledge, wisdom, intuitively felt unity of the universe.

आत्मज्ञान = knowledge of the self, consciousness of real self.

अपरोक्षअनुभूति = direct realisation

दुःखनिवृति = cessation of misery

ऋषिः = a sage, an inspired poet, a seer of the Vedic hymn, a singer of Sacred hymns

तापस = an ascetic, a hermit

मुनि = a monk, an ecstatic person, a saint, a holyman.

त्रि = three.

त्रिमुनि = the three grammarion : Pāṇini, Katyāyana and Patanjali.

साधु = perfect, straight, good, a good man, a noble man, a holy man, an honest well disposed person.

सन्यासः = abandonment, renouncing.

सन्यासिन् = one who renounce the world and its attachment

तपस्या = religious austerity, penance

तपस्विन् = a mendicant, devout, practising penance

आचार्य = teacher

त्यागः = forsaking, leaving, giving up, dissociation.

त्यागिन् = one who has given up, a donor, one who has resigned (worldly objects), who has renunciated his ego.

दर्शन = philosophy

दार्शनिक = philosopher

वैदिक = follower of the Vedas, brahmanical tradition derived from the Vedas, well-versed in the Vedas.

वैदांग = subsidiary treatises, Vedic study, auxiliary to the Vedas, limb of the Vedas.

शिक्षा = phonetics.

कल्प = ritual.

निरुक्त = etymology, analysis.

छन्दस = metre.

व्याकरण = grammar.

ज्योतिष = astronomy.

पुरुषार्थ = the goals of life, aspirations, aims.

धर्म = duties.

अर्थ = wealth, possession.

काम = desire.

मोक्ष = liberation, cessation of bondage, final emancipation.

धर्म is standing on the four main pillars : सत्य (truth), शील (good conduct, character, conducive action). श्रद्धा (faith, conviction), दान (charity).

श्रुति प्रस्थान = the revealed scripture, following the holy learning.

वेद = the body of knowledge, holy scriptures.

संहिता = collection of mantras, prayers and words of adoration, hymns.

ब्राह्मण = details of sacrificial rites, explanation of sacred knowledge.

आरण्यक = symbolic rites, philosophical writings composed in forest.

उपनिषद् = metaphysical enquiry, a class of philosophical composition, mystical treatises.

स्मृतिप्रस्थान = the remembered scripture, the way of remembered literature following the sacred tradition.

पुराण = legendary composition, a class of sacred texts, mythology.

साहित्य = literature.

इतिहास = history, narative, traditional account of former events.

शास्त्र = sacred treatise, manual of rules, manual of good counsel, religious or scientific book.

न्यायप्रस्थान = philosophical literature, the path of philosophy, following the method of reasoning exposition.

Philosophical Tradition	*Composer*
वैशेषिक	कनाद
न्याय	गोतम
सांख्य	कपिल
योग	पतंजलि
मीमांसा	जैमिनि
वेदान्त	व्यास (वादरायण?)

त्रिमूर्ति = the Hindu triad Brahmā, Vishṇu and Mahesvara

त्रित्व = three is one, <u>ब्रह्मा</u> <u>विष्णु</u> <u>महेश्वर</u>, a triad, the supreme triple principles (of one)

त्रयी = triple, three fold, a set of three things or presonalities, the three Vedas taken collectively.

शिव = auspicious

मृत्युंजय = the conqueror of death, an epithet of Śiva

महाकाल = a name of Śiva.

महादेव = the great God, name of Śiva

शंकर = Conferring happiness, name of Śiva.

त्रिशूल = a trident.

त्रिअंबक (त्रयंवक) = three eyes.

कुंडलिनी = coiling serpent.

(The symbol in Tantra) coiled serpent represents :

(*i*) The basic energy of living beings (in the microcosm);

(*ii*) cycles of time in the macrocosm.

Lord Śiva is the 'master of time and energy'. Śivamurti is adorned with snakes. Śiva is the conqueror of death so cobra which symbolises death is an ornament for him.

The letter pronounced by Lord Śiva is 'āgata' (आगत), that which goes to Parvati is 'gata' (गत) That which is established is known as 'mata' (मत). Things are known through words, it is 'jñāna' (ज्ञान) *i.e.*, knowledge is derived form the word. So it is known as 'āgama' (आगम). An Āgama deals with seven topics : cosmology, worship of God, destruction, Sādhanā, puraścārana, six forms of rites and four forms of meditation.

Word perpetuates and preserves the knowledge, working of words can be compared with a loom = 'tantra' (तंत्र).

Śiva's trident represents vairāgya (वैराग्य) jñāna (ज्ञान) and samādhi (समाधि).

त्रिपुरासूर = The ego in gross, subtle and causal bodies.

Śiva's three eyes see past, present and future. Three eyes also represent the sun, The moon and fire, reciprocally representing Iṛā (इडा) Pingalā (पिंगला) and suṣumanā (सुषुम्ना) nāris.*

Śiva is the Lord of the yogis (महायोगी), who dissolves the wrong senses of all diversities. Lord Śiva's vehicle (वाहन) is a bull named Nandi. Nandi represents 'dharma', in its four pillars : truth, purity, kindness and charity.

---

* Hindu symbology and essays, Swami Swahananda, pp. 25 Sri Ramakrishna math, Madras, 1983.

The sound of kettle drum (ḍamaru) is 'nāda brahman' stands for creation. Nataraja is 'The Lord of the stage'. The stage is the transitory world. The Lord tramples the demon of ignorance, the ego (अपस्मार).

Śiva Temples in Southern India

The five temples in Kanchipuram, Tiruvanaikavu, Kalahasti, Tiruvanmalai, Chidamvaram are representing five elements respectively : earth, water, air fire and ether.

योग = linking, yoking, certain philosophical point of view, concentration

लिंग = sign, emanation, manifestation, 'the state of existence standing as the sign'.

Linga	*Place*	*State*
श्री सोमनाथ	Somnath	Gujarat
श्री मल्लिकार्जुन	Śriśailam	Andhra Pradesh
श्री महाकाल	Ujjain (Avanti)	Madhya Pradesh
श्री ओंकारेश्वर	Indor	Madhya Pradesh
श्री केदारनाथ	Garoal	(Himalaya) Uttar Pradesh
श्री विश्वेश्वर	Varanasi	Uttar Pradesh
श्री वैजनाथ	Near Parle	Maharastra *
श्री नागेश्वर	Near okha	Gujrat +
श्री त्रयवंकेश्वर	Nasik road	Maharastra
श्री रामेश्वरसम	Near Dhanuskoti	Tamilnadu
श्री धृष्णेश्वर	Near Elora cave	Maharastra
श्री भीमाशंकर	Near Nanded	Maharastra +
*वैघनाथ	Deoghar	Jharkhand
वैजनाथ	Kangra	Himachal Pradesh

± There is a controvery regarding the locations and shrines.

The above mentioned are very important Śiva temples in India. Different manifestations of Lord Śiva = jyotirlinga ± स्वयंभु (selfmanifested).

आम्नाय = sacred tradition, observing traditional instructions

आम्ना = to regard, keep in mind, commit to memory, learn, to hand down traditionally

चतुराम्नाय पीठानि

	पूर्वाम्नाय	*पश्चिमाम्नाय*	*उत्तराम्नाय*
स्थानम	जगन्नाथपुरी (गोवर्द्धनमठ)	द्वारका (कालिकापीठम)	वदरिकाश्रम (ज्योतिर्मठ:)
देवता	जगन्नाथस्वामी-शक्ति विशालदेवी	सिद्वेश्वर-शक्ति भद्रकाली	श्रीमन्नरायण-शक्तिपूर्णगिरि
तीर्यम	महोदधि:	गोमती	अलकानन्दा
वेद:	ऋगवेद:	सामवेद:	अथर्ववेद:
आचार्य:	श्री हस्नामलकाचार्य:	श्री पदमपादाचार्य:	श्री तोढकाचार्य:
संप्रदाय	मागवल:	कितवल:	नन्दवल:
महावाक्यम्	प्रज्ञान ब्रह्म	तत्वमसि	अयमात्माब्रह्म
बिरुदावलि:	अरण्यम्, वनम्	तीर्थ:, आश्रम:	गिरि:, पर्वत:, सागर:

दक्षिणाम्नाय

स्थानम	श्रृंगोरि (शारदापीठम्)
देवता	विभाण्डकमुणि सेवित लिंगम वराहशक्ति श्री शारदादेवी
तीर्थम	तुंगभद्रा
वेद:	यजुर्वेद:
आचार्य	श्री सुरेश्वराचार्य:
संप्रदाय	भूरिवल:
महावाक्यम	अहम ब्रह्मास्मि
बिरूदावलि:	सरस्वती, पुरी, गिरि:, भारती, अरण्यम, तीर्थ: आश्रम:*

* This table was collected form Śaṅkara piṭham, Kaladi

The four important centers founded Śamkarācārya.

Saṁkara's famous theory of three levels of experience:

(*i*) illusory = pratibhāsika (apparent) = so long the object is perceived,

(*ii*) contradicted with absolute experience, it is finite, everchanging = vyavahārika (phenomenal/practical) = experience of waking life,

(*iii*) absolute = pāramārthika = infinite, exists eternally.

शिव · = auspicious.

बिरूदावलि = detailed panegyric.

दशनामी = the ten orders of monk.

सूत्र = a concise technical sentence.

वेदान्तसूत्र (ब्रह्मसूत्र) = the treatise on Vedanta, a philosophical text.

बाद्रायण (बादरायण) = the composer of the Brahmasutra.

योगसूत्र = the treatise on yoga, aphorisms of yoga.

पतंजलि = the composer of yogasutra.

यम = moral observance.

नियम = discipline.

आसन = proper sitting, posture.

प्राणायाम = breathing control.

प्रत्याहार = withdrawal of the sense.

धारण = concentration, awareness is focused on an object may be on the heart, on Om, one's chosen deity, concentrating awareness between the eyebrows.

ध्यान = meditation, unbroken flow of the mind.

समाधि = absorption, going beyond mind.

फल = result, fruit, consequence, reward.

उपेक्षा = overlooking, indifference, disregard.

चित्तवृत्ति = movements of mind, mind waves.

चित्तवृत्तिनिरोध = cessation of metal waves.

मैत्री = Friendliness.

करूणा = Kindly feeling, compassion.

मुदिता = feeling of happiness, contentment, delight .

प्रतिपक्षभावना = practising the opposite good thought.

अनुभव = experience, intuition (in Vedanta), feeling/ emotion (later).

अनुभवगम्य = realised in experience, apprehension.

अनुष्ठान = performance.

असत् = dishonesty, non-existence.

अन्तरंग = esoteric, internal, close, innercircle.

अकर्तृ = non-doer.

अन्त = end, nearest.

अपराध = sin.

अचिन्त्य = inconceivable.

अमित्र = an enemy, not a friend.

अम्बर = the sky.

अशुभ = inauspicious.

अभाव = scarcity, want, negation.

अहैतुकी = selfless, without any reason.

अद्रुह = free form melice, hate.

अद्रोहु = free form ill feeling.

अतिथि = guest.

अदिति = boundless, inexhaustible, the goddess Aditi, mother of the Ādityas and of the gods.

अर्चि = ray of light.

अर्चना = worship.

अपरिग्रह = acceptance only which is necessary.

अपवर्ग = libration.

अवस्था = the state, condition.

अभ्यास = practise, exercise, repeated action, following a discipline.

अमृत = nectar.

अद्वैत = non dual, unchanging, not two.

अद्वय = identity of spirit and matter, the ultimate truth.

अनवसाद = cheerfulness, optimism.

अभ्युदय = vigorous active life following the varnāśama dharma.

अभाव = non existence, absence, negation.

अव्यक्त = indiscrete, unmanifest, the primordial element.

अहुंकार = ego sense.

अहिंसा = non-injury.

आकाश = void, sky.

आख्यात = made known, declared, verb (in grammar).

आर्जभम = straightforwardness.

आप = water.

आचार = the method, custom.

आहवान = invocation, welcome, calling.

आनन्द = bliss, ecstasy.

आश्रय: = shelter, substratum, a resting place.

आस्तेय = non-stealing.

आराधना = propitiating, worship, adoration.

आसक्ति = attachment, addiction.

आस्तिक = belief in the presence of divine power, orthodox, who accepts the authority of the Vedas.

इन्द्रिय = organs.

इनि = thus.

इला = the earth.

इतिहास = history, accounts of former events.

उपदेश = good counsel, instruction, advice.

उपासना = homage, service, worship.

उपासक = a worshipper.

उपसर्ग = indication, trouble, problem, symptom, supplement, prefix suffix (grammar).

उपेक्षा = indifference, disregard.

एक = one, whole, undivided.

एकाग्र = one pointed, closely attentive.

ऐतिहय = tradition, legendary account.

ऐतिहासिक = an historian, one who is expert in ancient records.

ऐश्वर्य = wealth, the divine glory.

ओजस् = power, vituality, vigour, energy, lustre.

कर्ता = agent, doer, the supreme Agent.

कामना = desire, love, wish, affection.

कामरूप = taking form at will.

काम्य = desirable, agreeable, amiable.

कामधेनु = milch cow (fulfiller of all desires).

कल्याण = auspicious, beneficial, welfare.

काय: = the body, assemblage.

कैवल्य = emancipation.

कार = maker, doer (at the end of word), an agent.

कारा = a prison, confinement.

क्रियाशक्ति = the power of action.

कारण = cause, reason, ground, means.

कारूणिक = compassionate.

कार्य = work, duty, business to be performed.

काल = black colour, a space of time.

केवल = oneness, only.

कल्पना = fancy, imagination.

काल्पनिक = supposed, imaginary.

केल्श = affliction, hardship.

क्षत्र = rulership.

केतु = banner.

क्षेत्र = field.

क्षिप्त = wild.

ख = the sky.

खेचर = a bird.

गनपति = Lord of the people.

गुण = attribute, quality, virtue.

गुहा = cave, a secret place.

गोप = a cowherd, milkman.

गोपी = a milk maid.

गुह्य = mysterious, concealed, secret instruction.

गोविन्द = Kṛṣṇa, the lord of (cow herds) cows.

चिंत = the mind.

चिन्तभूमि = the mind, being in the heart.

चैतन्य = consciousness.

चरम = ultimate.

चरित्र = conduct, disposition, character

जाति = the form of existence marked by birth, race, family, lineage, a caste.

जड = dull, frigid, motionless.

जिष्णु = victorious.

जाग्रत = waking state.

ज्योति = light, glow.

ज्योतिस = lustre, brightness.

ज्योत्स्ना = moon light.

जप = repeating prayers.

जय = conquest, victory.

जैन = Jaina tradition.

तप = heat, penance, religious austerities.

तर्पण = offering of water to the deceased ancestors (पितृयज्ञ).

तत्व = truth, first principal, thatness, constituents that build up the creation.

तंत्र = a loom, a string, a cord, system, framework, theory.

तितिक्षा = endurance, fortitude.

त्यक्त = forsaken, abandoned.

तितीर्षु = desirous of crossing.

तिथि = a lunar day.

तेंजस = flame, glow, light, power.

तिमिर = darkness, gloomy.

तीर = a shore.

तीर्थ = place of pilgrimage, way, road to a river.

तृप्त = satisfied.

त्रय = triple, threefold.

त्राणं = protection.

त्रातृ = a protector, saviour.

तोयं = water.

तोष = satisfaction, pleasure, contentment.

त्रेना = the three sacred fire.

त्रिशूल = a trident.

त्रिलोकं = the three worlds.

तृष्णा = thirst, desire.

दया = compassion.

दान = charity, gift.

दाहिकाशक्ति = the power of burning.

दाहन = reducing to ashes.

दिव्य = divine, celestical.

द्रव्य = substance, object.

धन्वंतरि = the author of Ayurveda, the physician of the God.

धातृ = creator, supporter.

धरित्री = the earth.

धाम = adobe, a sacred site.

धात्री = mother, a nurse, foster mother.

धान्य = corn, rice.

धारण = retention, keeping.

धरणी = the earth, supporter.

धीरता = patience, composed nature.

ध्यान = meditation, constant flow of the mind to one object (profound thought).

धेनु = a cow, milch cow.

धृष्णु = bold.

धैर्य = calmness, stability, patience.

ध्वनि = sound, echo.

ध्रुव = parmanent, unchangeable.

ध्वान्त = darkness.

नक्त = night.

नक्षत्र = a star, constellation.

नग = a mountain.

नाग = a snake, the cobra, serpent demon.

नट = a dancer, an actor.

नाथ = master, lord.

नाद = a loud sound.

नाम = a name, a substantive (in grammer).

नारायण = primaeval water, the resting place, goal of naras.

नर = a man.

नास्तिक = one who disregard the vedic authority, an atheist, non believer.

नारी = a women.

निपात = incidental addition (in grammer).

नियम = regulation.

नि:श्रेयस = the path of perfection, metaphysical enquiry.

निवृत्ति = abstinence and asceticism.

निरोध = cessation.

नम्रता = modesty.

निद्रा = sleep (vacant state of mind).

निर्गुण = without qualities, the absolute.

निस्तार = passing over, acquitance, release.

नीहार = fog, mist, dew.

न्याय = method, rule, fitness, justice.

न्याय्य = just, right, equitable at law.

नित्य = constant, uninterrupted, eternal.

निषिद्व = prohibited, forbidden.

नैमित्तिक = occasional.

पंक्ति = a line, series.

पति = a master, husband.

पत्नी = a wife.

परिशिष्ट = an appendix, a supplement, left over, remaining.

पद्म = a lotus.

पथिकृत = path finder.

पदार्थ = substance, a thing, object.

पद्धति = manual, guide.

पावक = purifier.

पृथिवी = the earth, soil.

पार्थिव = earthly, terrestrial.

पूजनं = worshipping, adoring.

पुण्य = virtue, merit, sacred.

पूर्ण = full, whole, complete.

पुर = place, abode, a city, the body (psycho-physical existence).

पुंडरीक = a white lotus.

पुरूष = a man, male person, mankind, the primaeval man, the supreme being.

पूज्य = venerable, respectable.

प्रकाश = display, manifestation, appearance, reveal.

परम = greatest, the best, supreme, extreme.

पुरानी = ancient, primeval.

पुष्दि = nourishment, growth.

प्रचेत = wise.

प्रथम = primal, first.

प्रज्ञा = wisdom.

प्रणव: = the Om mantra, the sacred syllabus.

प्रतीति = conviction, perception.

प्रत्यवाय = an offence.

प्रमाण = proof, testimony, valid cognitive states, evidence.

प्रवचन = exposition, teaching the scriptures.

प्रयोग = manual.

प्रवृत्ति = tendency, inclination, natural inclination, instinct, propensity.

प्रस्तावना = beginning, introduction, commencement.

प्रेम = love, affection.

प्रसाद = serenity, composure, food offered to deity.

प्रेय = desired.

प्रेष्ठ = beloved.

प्रमाद = negligence, blunder, mistake.

प्रमूढ = bewildered, perplexed, ignorent.

पेय = a drink.

पयस = water, milk.

प्रभविष्णु = all powerful.

बीज = seed, germ.

बीजावस्था = the germinal state.

वल = vigour.

वर्ण = colour, script, caste.

वस्तु = object, substance, a reality, exciting thing.

वरूण = name of an Aditya.

वरिष्ठ = noblest.

वशी = mastery.

वात = air, wind.

वायु = air, vital breath.

वाधित = contradicted.

वाघकाभाव = non-contradicted.

वामा = woman.

वासना = desire, a wish, expectation.

वसुंधरा = the earth, holding riches.

वाह्यिक = exterior, outer, outward.

वहिरंग = external, nonessential, strange.

विचार = discussion, metaphysical exposition, deliberation, thought, decision, consideration, Judgement.

विधि = injunction, compulsion, obligatory action, method, means.

विपर्यय = false knowledge, inversion, contrariety.

विवेक = discrimination, conscience.

वृन्द = multitude, assemblage.

विमोक = longing for God.

विवर्त = transfiguration, forms which are apparently real

विभुति = miraculous power, prosperity, welfare

विविदिषा = desire to know.

विक्षेप = distraction, perplexity, waving.

विक्षिप्त = unsteady, agitated.

विकल्प = alternative, option.

विन्द = finding, getting, group, a flock.

विराज = manifestation, splendour.

विषय = subject, topic, a thing, matter, a concern.

वृन्दा = tulsi, basil.

विश्व:देव = the lord of the universe.

विश्वकर्मा = architect, the divine architect, accomplishing everything.

वीर्य = valour, performance, prowess.

वुद्धि = intelligence, discriminating faculty

वृत्ति = mental states, waves, process, stipend.

वैराग्य = indifference to worldly objects, discriminating wordly pleasure.

वैश्वानर = agni, the fire god, omnipresent, all commanding.

व्यवहारिक = mundane, every day use.

वौद्ध = followers of Buddha, Buddhist tradition.

व्रत = self dedication, a vow, austerity.

व्रज्या = wandering about.

वेदगामिनी = vedic way.

विश्वम्भर = all preserving.

भव = worldly existence, name of Śiva, the world, well being.

भवानी = name of Durga, consort of Bhava.

भग = divine lustre.

भर्ग = glory.

भद्र = good, well mannered, kind, gracious.

भजन = service, worship.

भवद्वेष = abandoning worldly attachment.

भवभय = fear of mundane existence, the cycle of birth and death.

भाष्य = commentary.

भिषक = physician.

भावात्मक = positive.

भावना = thought, imagination, conception, supposition.

भू = arising, becoming, existing.

भूमि = soil, ground.

भूमिका = preface, a step.

मनस = the mind, recording (impression) organ.

महान = splendour.

महार्घ्य = precious.

मित्र = friend.

मुक्ति = release, total exhaustion of merits and demerits, freedom.

मोह = attachment.

मार्ग = way, path.

मार्गशीर्ष = the months of December January, māgha.

यज् = to adore, honour.

यजुंस = veneration, a sacrificial prayer.

यजमान = a sacrificer.

युवा = young, handsome, strong, a young man.

युवती = a young woman, youthful.

रव = noise, sound, a roar, thunder.

रवि = the sun.

रस: = sap, juice, fluid.

रूद्र = terrific, howling, dreadful

रूप = form, a shape.

रथः = a chariot, a carriage.

रथी = a chariot driver, a coachman, a guide.

लीला = play, divine sport.

लक्ष्मी = good fortune, the goddess of wealth, prosperity.

लता = a creeper.

ललित = charming, gentle.

लोकायत = materialistic, materialism, cārvāka philosophy.

लोकसंग्रह = welfare of the world.

लीला = play, amusement.

लोभ = greed, covetousness.

लोलुप = ardently longing, greedy.

शक्ति = energy, strength, repository of energy, female counterpart, potency, God's own power.

शक्र = Indra, powerful, mighty.

शंका = alarm, fear.

शंकर = name, of śiva, auspicious, conferring happiness.

शब्द = sound, word, speech, language.

शम = tranquillity, restraint of passion, quietness of mind.

शंम्पा = lightning.

शान्त = calm, undisturbed, peaceful.

शिव = gracious, benevolent, benign, "in whom all things lie".

शिवानी = Pārvati, Durga.

शिशु = a child, infant.

शिष्य = a disciple, pupil.

शिष्द = disciplined, educated, cultured man.

शील = good conduct, manner.

शुचि = pure, bright.

शुद्ध = clean, holy, faultless.

शोभा = beauty.

शुभ = good, handsome, auspicious.

शुभ्र = shining, radiant, camphor, rocksalt.

शून्य = non existent, vacant, empty, absolute negation, void, nothingness.

शूर = a hero, valiant, brave.

श्याम = dark blue colour.

श्यामा = night, darknight, a darkwomen.

श्रद्वा = faith, trust, respect, conviction.

श्री = beauty, grace, wealth (homorific affix to names of persons and books etc.).

श्रुति = hearing, rumour, holy learning, the ear.

श्रेयस = most preferable, felicity, the best.

श्रमण = a Buddhist ascetic

श्रीमत् = dignified (a respectful affix to revered names of person).

श्रेष्ठ = the best, most splendid.

श्लाघा = praise, self praising, boasting.

संयम = restrain, control.

संयोग = conjunction.

संकल्प = particular desire, a solemn vow, will.

शिव संकल्प = moral guidance, good will.

सत् = honesty, existence.

सत्त = balance, harmony.

संशय = doubt.

संहार = ruin, destruction.

संवाद = information, news, message.

सगुण = with quality.

समाधि = absorption, trance, union..

समिध = wood for sacrifical fire.

संवित = consciousness, knowledge.

समत्त = balance, equality, equanimity

संस्कार = old potencies, impressions, conception, reformation.

संस्कृत = refined, polished, cultivated, the Sanskrit language.

साधना = discipline, 'means to an end', accomplishment.

सविशेष = distinguishing, superior, most deserving, detailed.

सिद्धि = highest end, attainment, fulfilment.

सम्राढ = emperor.

सत्संग = good company, association with noble people.

सभा = meeting, congregation, an assembly.

समिति = group, union, association.

सुनीति = goodness, good conduct, excellent policy.

सुपथ = right path.

सुपर्ण = beautiful winged bird.

समदर्शन = perception of equality.

सोम = the moon, juice of a plant.

सौम्य = handsome, lovely, charming.

स्वप्न = dream.

स्वयम् = oneself.

सृष्टि = creation.

स्थिति = sustenance.

स्वरूप = real nature.

स्वयमप्रकाश = self luminous, self evident.

स्वर्ग = heaven.

स्वर्ण = gold.

स्वस्ति = bliss, prosperity, an exclamation of benediction.

स्वस्तिक = a mystical mark denoting good luck.

साक्षी = witness, spectator, the inner spirit.

स्वादु = tasteful, delicious.

स्वामिन् = an owner, master.

स्वाहा = an oblation, offering, an exclamation, name of the wife of Agani.

स्वैर = self willed, unrestrained.

स्वैरिणी = an adultress, uncontrolled women, harlot.

हर = removing, name of Śiva, divisor, denominator (in arithmetic).

हरि = name of viṣṇu.

हरित = green, yellowish, tawny colour.

हरिद्रा = turmeric.

हिंसा = injury, harm.

हिम = cold, forsty.

हेतु = cause, reason.

हिमानी = a mass of snow.

हिरण्यगर्भ = name of Brahman, born from a golden egg.

हर्ष = delight, joy, rapture.

Some Examples of Word Formation

(The verbal derivatives *i.e.*, Kṛdanta) = affixes are added to the roots.

धातु = (Roots)

√अर्च = to worship

√कृ = to do

√गॄ = to utter

√गै = to sing

√ग्रह = to take

√द्रश = to see

√जन् = to he born

√धृष् = to be bold, polish

√दीक्ष = to dedicate one self

√पा = to protect

√भज = to worship

√युज = to join, to unite

√मन्त्र = to counsel

√सृज = to create

√स्तु = to praise, to glorify

√स्पृह = to desire

√हु = to sacrifice

√हन् = to kill

√श्रु = to hear

√मन् = to think

√मुच् = to realise, release

√शक = to be able

कृत् प्रत्यय Suffix/Affix Added Directly to the Roots

क्तिन् (=क्ति/ति)

मज्+क्ति = भक्ति, devotion, faith

मुच्+क्ति = मुक्ति, release, freedom in the ordinary sense, form the point of view of philosophy and religion it may mean 'Kamanās'; release from accumulated merits and demerits, disappearance of name and form distinction, enlightenment, the knowledge of unity etc.

कृ+ति = कृति

श्रु+ति = श्रुति, ear

स्तु+ति = स्तुति, praise

गै+ति = गीत, song

शक्+ति = शक्ति, power

णक (= अक)

गै+अक = गायक, singer

पठ्+अक = पाठक, reader

मुच्+अक = मोचक, liberator

तृ+अक = तारक

क्नु (=नु)

धृष्+नु = धृष्णु bold

अनट् (=अन)

Words (nominalbase) formed with this suffix are neuter.

मन्+अन = मननम् minding, Thinking

दृश+अन = दर्शनम् seeing

क्त (=त)

कृ+त = कृत done

श्रु+त = श्रुत heard

स्तु+त = स्तुत praised, glorified

युज+क्त = युक्त united

भज+क्त = भक्त devotee

मुच+क्त = मुक्त released, free

मन्+त = मत opinion, viewpoint

Potential Participles

तव्य, अनीय, णत्, यत् and क्यप् (used in passive voice).

तव्य, अनीय

(In the sense must be/ought to be)

कृ+तव्य = कर्तव्य ought to be done

सृज+तव्य = सष्टव्य ought to be/must be created

श्रु+तव्य = श्रोतव्य must be heard

ग्रह+अनीय = ग्रहणीय fit to be taken

कृ+अनीय = करणीय ought to do

पठ+अनीय = पठनीय must be read

अच्चि+अनीय = अर्च्चनींय ought to be worshipped

There are Various Kinds of Affixes

उणादि प्रत्यय

मन् (मः)

हु+मन् = होमः sacrifice

सू+मन् = सोमः moon

धृ+मन् = धर्मः duty, virtue, religion

नु

भा+नु = भानुः sun

सू+नु = सूनुः son

विष+नु = विष्णुः

नि

अन्ग्+नि = अग्निः fire

वह+नि = वह्णि fire

भ

द्र+भ = दर्भः kusha grass

ऋ+भ = अर्भः child

इ+भ = इभः elephant

गृ+भ = गर्भः womb, embryo, foetus

उनन् (उन)

ऋ+उनन् = अरूणः tawny, purple colour, the sun

ऋज्+उनन् = अर्ज्जुनः the third son of pandu, a kind of medicinal tree

तृ+उनन् = तरूण youth, tender, fresh

कृ+उनन् = करूण pathetic, melancholy

व

गृ+व = गवर्वः pride

श्रृ+व = शवर्वः śiva

वन् (व)

शि+वन् = शिवः

ह्रस्+वन् = ह्रस्व short

स्तोत्राञ्जलि

SURYA PRAṆĀM (सूर्यप्रणाम)

ओम् जवाकुसुम संकाशंकाश्यपेयं महाद्युतिम्।
ध्वान्तारिम् सर्वपापघ्न प्रणतोस्मि दिवाकरम्।।

(*from Pāṇḍavagita*)

ओम् = अ उ म

It contains the Vedic concept of cosmic power : all pervading Brahman is referred to which causing the process of creation, sustenance and dissolution perpetually.

ओम् is नाद in Tantra, meaning 'cosmic vibration'.

जवा कुसुम सम काशम

जपा = saffron colour blossom

जवा = saffron

जवाकुसुम = reddish china rose

कुसुम = blossom, flower

सम = like, as, similar to

काशम् = look brilliant, shining, to be visible, appear = the golden glow on the horizon (in the eastern sky), The luminous sum.

काश्यपेयम् = The son of Kashyapa

अयन = descended from, path

महाद्युतिम् = majestic splendour

= with illuminating lustre, the source of life, the source of light and energy (The Sun)

अपन्य = Offspring descendent, progeny

घ्वांतं = darkness (तम)

अरि = an enemy

= remover of all darkness

तमोनाशन, तमोविनाशी = घ्वान्तारिम् तमः अपहन = तमोपहः (sun)

Mind, body and the whole world get energy form sunlight.

सर्व = all

पाप = sin, vice, inauspicious

घ्न = destroyer of all impurity, inauspiciousness

प्रणतः = bowing to, bending

अस्मि = I am

प्रणतोस्मि = I bow down to, salutation to

दिवाकरः = the sun

धातु = (Roots)

√ध्वन् 'dark'

√नम् 'to bow'

√सृ 'to move', to go

√सू 'to incite', to impel

√अस् 'to be', to exist

√हन् 'to kill'

√कृ 'to do'

उपसर्ग (Prefix)

प्र

प्रत्यय (Suffix/Affix)

त

√ध्वन् - ध्वान्त

√नम् - नत, प्र+नत = प्रणत

क्यप

√सृ+क्यप/सू+क्यप = सूर्यः (सरति आकाशे इति सूर्यः) sun

√अस+मि = अस्मि Ist person singular

√कृ preceded by दिवा = दिवाकरः (दिवा करोतिति) The sun
preceded by prabhā = प्रभाकरः

दिवा - day, प्रभा - light, radiance

√हन - पापंहन्ति = पापघ्न हन + ति

3rd person singular हुन्ति

उम जवा कुसुम सम काशम् काश्यप अपन्यम् महा द्युतिम्।
ध्वान्त अरिम् सर्व पापघ्न प्रणन अस्मि दिवाकरम्॥

Praṇam mantra is a hymn, a song of praise, an obeisance, salutation.

Source : Pāṇḍava Gītā

ŚIVĀṢṬAKASTOTRAM (शिवाष्टकस्तोत्रम्)

प्रभुमीशमनीशमशेष गुणं गुणहीनमहीशगराभरणम्।
रणनिर्जितदुर्जयदैन्यपुरं प्रणमामि शिवं शिवकल्पतरूम्॥

प्रभु - Lord, master

ईश - God, the supreme spirit, a name of Śiva

अनीश(अन+ईश) absolute, non-Iśa, (अनीश), superior, paramount

अशेष - boundless, various, infinite

गुण - quality

गुणहीन(=निर्गुण) - without any attribute, qualityless

अहि - serpent

ईश - king, lord

गर - venom

आभरण - ornament, decoration

रण - fight, battle, war

निर्जित(निः+जित) = completely overpowered

निः - complete, fully

जित - conquered, won, overcome

दैत्य - demon, wicked

पुर - city, dominion, citadel

दैत्यपुर - demon's dominion, dungeon

प्रणमामि - I bow, I adore

शिव - Śiva, The auspecious, kind Lord

शिवकल्पतरू - auspecious wish yielding tree

In this couplet Lord Śiva in the object of reverence, all other expressions are attributes to the Lord. The word śivam indicates the accusative marker (विभक्ति) m (म), accordingly. The qualitative marker appears in other expressions as well (objective completment).

Some words are neuter so they appear with the marker म which can indicate both nominative and accusative sense in singular number.

अष्टक – a set of eight, a collection of eight (here क is a secondary affix)

स्रोत्र – verses, panegyric, a hymn of praise

प्रत्यय (कृत – primary affixes added to verbs) The following nominal is derived form the root स्तु by means of adding the affix.

ष्ट्न (=त्र)

स्तु+त्र = स्रोत्र

स्तौति अनेन स्तोत्रम् (verses to be sung)

श्री शंकराचार्य प्रणीत Composed by Sri Samkarācārya

प्रभुभ्, ईशन् अनीशम्, अशेष-गुणम्, गुणहीनम्, अहि-ईश-गर-आभरणम् रण-निर्जित-दैत्य-पुरम्, प्रणमामि शिवम् शिवकल्पतरूम्॥

The first couplet from the śiva aṣṭak-stotram.

BHAVANI ĀSṬAKAM (भवन्याष्टकम्)

न तातो न माता न वन्धुर्न नप्ता
न पुत्रो न पुत्री न भृत्यो न भर्ता।

न जाया न विद्या न वृत्तिर्ममैव
गतिस्त्वम् गतिस्त्वम् तत्वमेका भवानि॥

न – no.

तातः – a father.

माता – a mother.

बन्धुः – a friend, relation.

नप्ता – a grand child, grandson.

पुत्रः – a son.

पुत्री – a daughter.

जाया – a wife.

विद्या – knowledge.

वृत्ति – vocation.

मम – mine (अस्मद genetine singular).

एव – indeed, only.

गतिः – resort, destination, refuge, shelter.

त्वम् – you (युस्मद nominative singular).

त्वम् – you (युस्मद nominative singular).

एका – alone.

भृत्यः – servant, dependent.

भता – master .

भवानी – mother goddess, devi Durga (भवस्य जाया भवानी) (भव = शिव, भव with feminine marker = भवानी).

भवानि - (address) O mother Bhavāni.

न जानामि दानं न च घ्यानयोगं
न जानामि तन्त्रं न च स्त्रोत्रमन्त्रम्।
न जानामि पूजां न च न्यासयोगं
गतिस्त्वम् गतिस्त्वम् त्वमेका भवानि॥

न - not.

जानामि - I know (present tense 1st person singular of ज्ञा).

ज्ञा - to know.

दान - The act of giving, charity, alms.

घ्यानयोग - meditation.

योग - The act of yoking, rite conducive to the yoga system. The means of attaining union with The Supreme Spirit.

तन्त्र - Theory, system, The System of mystical formularies, charms, incantation.

मन्त्र - divine formula, Vedic hymn, rituals.

स्तोत्र - laudation, prayer, a song of praise, holy name.

पूजा - worship.

न्यासयोग - renunciation, purification by proper invocation.

न - not, on.

च - and, also.

गतिस्त्वम गतिस्त्वम् न्वमेकाभवानि = Indeed you are the only refuse, O Mother Bhavani thou art my only shelter.

गतिः त्व्म = गतिस्त्वम्

त्वम् एकां = त्वमेको

भवानी अष्टकम् = भवन्याष्टकम्

The first (प्रथम) and the third (तृतीय) stanza (स्तवक) form the Bhavānī aṣṭakam, composed by Sri Samkaracarya (श्रीशंकराचार्य-रचित).

GANGASTOTRAM (गङ्गास्तोत्रम्)

देविसुरेश्वरि भगवति गङ्के त्रिभुवनतारिणि तरलतरङ्के।
शंकरमैलिनिवासिनि विमले मम मतिरास्तां तव पद कमले॥

देवी – a goddess, a female deity, name of Durga, name of Sarasvati, a respectful addressing term.

सुर – a god.

ईश्वरी – goddess, sakti, energy of the deity.

भगवती – adorable Devi with six divine qualities, a respectful addressing term.

गङ्गा – the river Gangas.

त्रि – three.

भुवन – world.

तारण – saviour.

तरल – fluid, liquid.

तरङ्ग - ripple, wave.

शंकर - Śiva.

मौलि - a tuft of hair on the head, the matted hair on the crown.

निवास - residence, dwelling place.

विमल - stainless, pure, beautiful.

मम - my, mine.

मति - mind, inclination.

आस्ताम - remain, be fixed, stay always, attended to, continue.

तव - your.

पद - foot.

कमल - lotus.

तरलतरङ्ग - wavy water course.

त्रिभुवन - the three worlds. (स्वर्ग, मर्त्य, पाताल)

स्वर्ग - the heaven.

मर्त्य - the earth.

पाताल - The last region of the seven, under the earth (water).

ममति: - my mind, intellect, mind waves, inclinations

मति: आस्ताम = मतिरास्ताम् mind (mind waves) continue to stay on, remain attached to.

तवपदकमले - to your lotus feet (=locative marker).

निवासिनि विमले – the embodiment of purity residing (dwelling) in Śiva's Locks.

गङ्गे = O mother Ganges

The marker ए (e) in विमके and गङ्गे is a kind of interjection showing respect.*

आस्ताम = third person Imperative tense of आस (to sit, to stay) with singular marker

Feminine Markers

आ, ई, ऊ, ति

The first couplet of Ganga stotram, Composed by Sri Samkaracarya (श्री शंकराचार्य प्रणीत)

---

* "It is sudden exclamation prompted by some strong feeling or emotion."

APARADHA KṢAMAPAṆA STORAM
(अपराधक्षमापणस्त्रोत्रम्)

प्रसीद भगवत्यमव प्रसीद भक्तवत्सते।
प्रसादं कुरू मे देविदुर्गे नमोऽस्तु ते॥

(The last couplet of the stotram)

अपराध – sin, offence, wrong doing.

क्षमा – pardon, forgiveness.

क्षमापण – asking for forgiveness, begging pardon.

प्रसाद – graciousness, serinity of disposition.

प्रसीद – be gracious.

भगवती – respectful addressing term, goddess, The Mother.

अम्बा – mother.

अम्ब – 'the great pervading principle of the universe', mighty (personified as Mother).

भक्त – devotee.

वन्सल – affectionate, kind, compassionate.

नम – a bow, salutation.

भग = ऐश्वर्य, वीर्य, यश, श्री, ज्ञान, वैराग्य

वान/वती = agentive suffix.

भगवान – The Lord, god.

भगवती – The Mother of the Universe.

कुरु – second person, singular, Imperative of कृ (to do).

अस्तु – third person, Singular, Imperative tense of अस् (to be).

ते – to you.

मे – me, to myself.

Wrong Doing : Imperfect reading, pronunciation, incorrect, indistinct utterances, omissions, misunderstanding or unable to follow the inner meaning. The purport is not received due to ignorance etc.

अम्बा – a name of Parvati (Devi).

अम्बु – water.

अम्बुज – Lotus, water born.

अम्बुद – cloud.

अम्बुधि – Ocean, Sea.

अम्बर – The sky.

The final portion of Devi-Māhātmya contains the Aparādha kṣamāpana stotram. Devi-Māhātmya or Durga-Saptaśati is a part of Mārkaṇḍeya Purāṇa.

शिवापराधक्षमापनस्तोत्रम

करचरणकृतं वाक्कायजं कर्मजं वा
श्रवणनयनजं वा मानसं वाऽपराधं।
विहितमविहितं वा सर्वमेतत् क्षमस्व
जय जय करूणाब्धे श्रीमहादेव शम्भो।।

कर – hand

चरण् – foot

कृतम् – done.

वाक – speech.

कायजम् – bodly acquired, in contact with body, caused by.

कर्मजम् – acquired by work, grown due to faulty action, improper act.

वा – or.

श्रवण – ear, hearing.

नयनजम् – acquired through eyes, sight, seeing.

मानसम् – by thinking, caused by ill thoughts.

अपराधम् – offence, mistake, wrongdoing, sin, omissions.

विहितम् – accumulated, acquired already.

अविहितम् – may be acquired in future, improper (action).

सर्वम् – all.

सर्वमेतत् – all these.

एतत् – this.

क्षमस्वं – you forgive (my lord, I pray, I beg).

क्षमा – pardon, forgiveness, a name of Devi Durga, forbearance.

जय – victory.

करुण – compassion, mercy, kindness, pity, tenderness.

अविद्ध – ocean, sea

करुणअव्धि – हे करूणा अव्धि = O, ocean of mercy (करूणासागर)

हे – a vocative particle.

अव्द्धे – addressing form.

श्री – fortune, beauty, a name of Lakṣhmi.

श्री – an honorific title.

श्रीयुत/श्रीयुक्त – endowed with fame, famous, illustrious.

श्री महादेव – The Divine Great God, Lord of the universe.

शम्भु – benevolent, existing for welfare, a name of śiva.

शम् – (An indeclinable word) - auspicious, pacified, calm.

भू – to be, to exist.

शम्+भू=शम्भु: – Śiva.

जात = grown, caused, born, arisen, produced.

क्षम: = a name of Śiva.

कर-चरण-कृत = done by hands and feet (caused by touching, doing etc.).

वाक-काय-जात = produced by (arisen from) body and speech.

श्रवंण-नयन-जात= acquired by hearing and seeing (caused by listening and sight through ears and eyes).

मानसम् = brought into existence by though.

अपराधम् = offence, crime, guilt, fault, sin, erring, error, mistake.

क्षमस्व = excuse me lord, you forgive me.

म = objective marker.

स्व = (indiclinable) Pronoun.

विहित = Ordained, possessed of (accumulated).

अविहित = may be incurred in future (birth) *i.e.*, what ever is accumulated in previous birth or will be incurred in future may be forgiven by the Gracious God.

करूणा अव्धे = O compassionate Master.

जय जय श्री महादेव शम्भो = Victory to the Benevolent Divine Great God.

Verse no. seventeen form the Śivāparādhakṣamāpana stotram composed by Śri Śamkarācāya. (श्रीशंकराचार्य प्रणीत शिवापराधक्षमापनस्तोत्रम्)

REFERENCES

1. Hymns and prayers compiled by Svāmi Pavitrānanda, Advaita Ashram, eighth impression 1988.
2. Stavakusumānjali edited by Svāmi Gambhirānanda, Udbodhan Karjālaya, Calcutta Tenth edition 1986.
3. Universal prayers by Svāmi Yatiswarānanda, Śri Ramakrishna Math, Mylapor, Madras 1977.
4. Mantrapuspam by Svāmi Devarupānanda, Ramakrishna Math, Khar, Mumbai First edition 1989.
5. Devi Māhatmyam (Glory of the Divine Mother) Svāmi Jagadīsvarānanda, Sri Ramakrishna Math, Madras 1953.

APPENDIX – A

THE CULT OF BHAKTI AND ŚRI CAITANYA

Kṛṣṇa is the complete and essential manifestation of God.

Kṛṣṇastu Svayam Bhagavān

He is attainable through the path of bhakti, ahaituki bhakti 'unmotivated, spontaneous, selfness devotion'; this is the tenet of Caitanya school of vaiṣṇavism.

The devotional attitude was expressed in Śruti. It can be traced form several expressions in the Vedic hymns and Upanisads. Through the intuitive faculty of mind and intensifying emotion human psychobiological components can be transcended, such transformed personalities impart a great influence on human society. Sri Caitanya was such a transformed personality, whose influence was tremendous in the eastern region of the country during the late medieval period.

In this paper I intend to provide a short discussion of the bhakti cult concentrating on the philosophy and religious doctrine of the Caitanya school of Vaiṣṇavism. Also I shall attempt to portray a bare outline of the life story of that great personality and to look briefly on the impact of Caitanya Vaiṣṇavism in Bengal.

Śri Kṛṣṇa Caitanya (or Gaurānga Mahāprabhu as he is lovingly remembered by the people) a Śankarite ascetic accelerated the spiritual awakening of Bengal and Orissa in the sixteenth century A.D. His teaching and activities stirred the social religious and cultural life of these provinces. Most of his close associates and contemporary followers took him as a God incarnated personality. It is a fervent belief of the Caitanya vaiṣṇavas in Bengal that Śri Caitanya was an incarnation of Rādha and Kṛṣṇa in one physical form. His life involved a performance of self-transfiguration and his mission was to share the taste of divine love with the fellow human beings. His personality enriched the collective subconscious plane to such a great extent that for centuries Rādha-Kṛṣṇa lore and his life story became the alluring theme of songs, dance literary compositions and art of the region.

1. The Bhāgavata religion came to the eastern region during the Gupta period. Vaiṣṇavism in this region seems to have received a stimulating incentive during the Sena kings of Bengal. Jayadeva composed 'Gita Govinda' in 12th century at the court of Lakṣhmana Sena. Before the advent of Śri Caitanya emotional ferver seems to have been blended in vaiṣṇavism, which took a definite shape in him.

The doctrine of śraddhā (faith) which is professed in the Upaniṣads in a course of time flourished in the Bhāgavata-dharma as bhakti. Through the intellect and metaphysical abstraction man realise the One as Brahman. The Upanisad says :

om purṇam adah purṇam idam
purṇāt purnamudacyate
purṇasya purṇamādāya purṇamevāvasisyate.

It expresses the realisation of the infiniteness and the oneness. Through devotion that One becomes the Supreme Deity, in this way man's spiritual aspiration is satisfied. The Nāsadiya Sukta recommends to visualize the Absolute Reality' in the depth of heart.

sato bandhum a-sati nir-avindam
hṛdi pratisya kavayo manisa.

In several texts the basic identity between the Brahman and the Supreme Deity is represented, the concept of bhakti evolved.

The Bhagavad Gita, Śrimad Bhāgavatam and Bhāgavata Purāna reveal Kṛṣṇa as the Parama Brahman, Bhagavān, Kṛṣṇastu Svayam Bhagavān, Kṛṣṇa is the self existent reality, says Bhāgavantam. And the Śrimad-Bhāgavata is considered to be the mature fruit of the Vedas :

nigama kalpatoror galitam phalam.

The Bhagavad Gīta expands the divine nature of Śri Kṛṣṇa :

avajananti mām muḍha mānusim tanumāśritam
param bhavam ajānanto mama bhutavahesvaram.

Absorbing the Vedic tradition, pronouncing the identity of Kṛṣṇa-vasudeva the Supreme Deity with the Brahman the Bhāgavata-dharma flourished, and propagated the attitude of bhakti. It had been established before the fourth century B.C. The term bhakti is mentioned in Nirukta, the etymological treatise composed by Yāska, who flourished before Pāṇini.

The Taittiriya-Āranyaka identifies Viṣṇu and Kṛṣṇa as one :

nārāyaṇāya vidmahe vāsudevāya dhimahi
tan no viṣṇuh procodayāt.

Also it records the merger of the Bhāgavata cult and the Pañcarātra cult. Thus resulted in the emergence of a general stream of vaiṣṇavism, in which four prominent schools were developed in the medieval period with the teachings, adoption of the principles and exposition of the religion by Ramanuja, Nimbarka, Madhva and Vallabha. The Caitanya school is developed later.

2. Śri Caitanya's message is to value the simplest way of life in the process of spiritual understanding, the mode of worship is to intensify the mental attitude to the object of worship. The key for self realization and God realization is devotion. The human life has a meaningful purpose to serve offering oneself to the loving service of the Lord who is the source and the goal of all living entities. A spiritual aspirant has to develop a sense of extreme tolerance and forbearance in his behaviour. The eight Sanskrit verses composed by Śri Kṛṣṇa Caitanya reveal his imagination, aspiration, feeling and conviction. These verses are the gist of his teachings and the philosophy of his divine emotionalism. Śri Caitanya's physical expressions and activities were expression of his inner spirit. His teachings were enlivened by his own experiences and realization. He sought God in the mādhurya aspect - seeking an intimate relationship. His mystical experience and sincere adoration were essentially personal, he considered himself as a seeker after Kṛṣṇa, and he wanted to share the blissful joy with others. His divine personality inspired many, he was like a living faith to his associates and followers. People became his devotees the sect grew around him, he did not make effort to build an organisation or thrust his views strongly upon anybody. His personality, wide views and simple mode of worship enthused some of his learned followers to systematise, and elaborate the doctrine and philosophy of the sect on the basis of his teaching, monopolysing the eight verses, interpreting his mystical emotionalism in conformity with the Śrimad Bhāgavatam and other texts.

The verse one says :

cetodarpaṇa mārjanam bhavamahādābāgnirvā-panam, sreyah kairavacandrikā vitaram vidyā badhu-jivanam.
ānandāmbudhi bardhananm pratipadam purṇā-mṛtāsvādam,
sarbātmasmapanam param vijayate śrikṛṣṇasaṃ-kīrtanam.

Glorify the name of Śrikṛṣṇa, the singing of the name cleanses the mirror of the mind. The singing extinguishes the 'conflagration of worldlyness'. It is the best, it is like the bright cool moonlight. It is stimulating and beautiful like the prime of youthful age. It increases the felling of blissful ocean of joy. Every word is relishable, it is all satisfying, all senses and sentiments are satisfied by uttering the name of Kṛṣṇa, it gives the taste of heavenly nector.

The fourth verse expresses his spiritual aspiration :

na dhanam na janam na sundarīm kavitā ba jagadisha kāmaye,
mama janmani janmanisvare bhava tādbhaktirahi tuki tvayī.

I pray not for wealth, company of men or beautiful women for self and sense gratification, nor do I desire for power. I long for, O Lord, an attitude of unqualified-spontaneous devotion to you in all my births.

The seventh verse is a description of Śri Rādhā in separation. Śri Caitanya himself exactly expressed the same sort of feeling in spiritual ecstasy. This verse signifies his inner spirit :

yugāitam nimeṣena cakhṣuṣā pravṛṣāitam,
śunyāitam jagat sarvam govinda viraheṇa me.

On account of separation form Govinda, a moment seems to be like a decade to me, my eyes do not cease to sheding tears; the entire world appears to be void to me.

The third verse says :

> **tṛinādapi sunīcena taroriba sahiṣṇuna,**
> **amāninā mānadena kirtaniya sadā harih.**[1]

Sing the glory of the Lord, 'be more humble, than a blade of grass, forbearing like a tree... rendering honour where honor is due.'

These verses give us an idea of Caitanya Mahāprabhu's teachings and conviction. He introduced a mode of simple chanting, devotional singing and dancing as a vehicle for spreading the spiritual message to the masses. All his biographers mention that the handsome ascetic left a stimulating impression on the people by his enthusiasm, simple worship, ecstatic singing and absorbed emotional expression. His charm inspired such scholarly and powerful persons like Advaita, Vāsudeva Sārbabhouma, Rupa, Sanatana, Prakasananda, Rāy Rāmananda and king Pratāparudra of Orissa.

At Puri for seven days Vāsudeva Sārbabhauma discussed the Vedanta philosophy with Śri Caitanya. He remained unsatisfied, he said 'eha bājhya āge kaho ār' - this is superficial, tell me something deeper than that. Sārbabhouma could not satisfy him with his scholarly exposition but he fell under the divine charm of the young sannyasi and became his disciple.

2.1. Form the biographical records we find that Śri Caitanya's name before entering into the ascetic order was Visvambhara Miśra, also he was called by the name Gourānga, Nirmāi. He was born in February 1486 at

Navadvipa, which was a well known centre of learning at that time. Navadipe was a place where orthodox Smārta system, Tantra system were flourished at the same time. Smārta Raghunandana and Āgamvāgisa Krisnānanda were Gourānga's elder contemporary. His parents Jagannath Miśra and Saci Devi were pious Brahmin of Vaiṣṇava faith. He had a brother who embraced monastic order and left home. His elderly parents were frighten that Nimāi might follow the path of his elder brother. They did not want to send Nimāi to school. Nimāi went to school later and at the age of 22 he was reputed as a scholar and a teacher, he was married to Lakṣmi, the daughter of a scholar of Navadvipa and set up a ṭol. Shortly he went to East Bengal and Sylhet in Assam, made an extensive tour in that region. On his return he got the news that Lakṣhmi Devi died of snake-bite. Soon he had to marry Viṣṇupriya, the daughter of Sanātana Miśra a pundit of Navadvipa. In the mean time his father died and as a dutiful son Nimāi pandit went on a pilgrimage to the holy place of Gaya to perform the pindadana ceremony. There he took initiation in Kṛṣṇa Mantra form the emotional ascetic Īśvara Puri whom Nimāi tried to win over at Navadvip on a previous occasion. What happened no one knows, a religious awakening transformed him. Nimāi came back to Navadvip as completely a changed man. He lost interest in worldly things, he gave up his ṭol. He organised (samkirtana) collective chanting, singing in chorus the name of God and led procession in the town. This novel way turned many to God consciousness. Śri Gourānga's mission now was to give the taste of the heavenly bliss to the fellow human beings. He was overpowered by the mystical emotion and became Kṛṣṇa intoxicated. His increasing religious experience and ecstatic expression established his divinity. He was recognised as an incarnation of divine soul by Advaita and the small group of Vaiṣṇava devotees at Navadvipa. At the age of 24 Sri Gaurānga became a Samkarite ascetic with the name Kṛṣṇa Caitanya. Sannyasi Kṛṣṇa Caitanya was to his associates and followers Caitanya Mahāprabhu.

Sometimes in February-March of 1510 he embraced the monastic order and left for Puri leaving his young charming wife and aged mother at Navadvip. The first six years of his sannyasa were spent on a pilgrimage. He went to Śrirangam, Udipi, Somanath, Dwaraka, Prabhasapatan, Pandharpuri, Kāshi, and Vṛindavana. Wherever he went and stayed Śri Caitanya showed respect to all religious leaders of all the sects he visited and to all the temples, and his living faith left a stimulating impression on the Vaiṣṇava, community and the society at large. He wished to live at Vṛndavan but he agreed to settle at Puri on his mother's request. Puri is nearer than Vṛndavara to Bengal, and every year his Bengal followers used to meet him during the Car-Festival of Śri Jagannat Deity at Puri. The last 12 years of his life Śri Caitanya lived mostly in spiritual ecstasy, he departed form the world on 9th of July 1533.

2.2. The development of this divine personality convinced his associates and followers that he was the divine incarnation of Sri Rādha. His Buddhist followers took him as an incarnaton of Bhagvān Buddha.

Mahāprabhu opened the horizon of the orthodox Smarta system in the matter of religion. He removed the barrier of caste prejudice and social hierarchy in the congregational singing. An inward illumination does not depend on individual's status of birth or sex distinction. An intuitive awakening can come through the intensified mental attitude. A simple, sincere attitude can be cultivated by individuals irrespective of caste and sex; for cultivation of such attitude intellectual capacity high rank and status etc. are nothing but superficial accessories. Mahāprabhu simplified the mode of worship, gave scope to all to participate and accepted non-Hindus as well. He never encouraged to monopolize the spiritual leadership on the basis of caste superiority although he never interfered with the established social order in social matter. His famous utterance expresses his thoughts :

> **nāham vipro na ca narapati nāpi vaisya na sudra novā varni na ca grihapatirno banasthayatirvā kintu pradyonnikhila paramānanda purṇa-mṛtabdhe gopibhrtuh padakamalayordāsa dāsānudāsah.**[2]

I do not belong to any caste, nor do I have a status of any ashrama, but I have taken refuge to the Lord of the universe who is ever blissful. I am a servant's servant of the beloved Master of the gopies.

2.3. At times when the alien rule and the orthodox Brahmanism both were dominant and oppressing, Mahaprabhu brought the message of complete freedom in the religious life, to some extent in the social life also. I have already mentioned that the incentive for inward lookingness and the cultivation for tolerent and respectful behaviour is to be found in the Śikṣāṣṭaka. He imparted a positive influence on the society by allowing the women, the members of the lower caste and non-Hindus to join in the congregration and in group singing. The members of the lower castes and the women got the rare opportunity to participate jointly together with the higher caste people. And that rouse a kind of social solidarity which was unknown in the stratified Brahmanical society. In fact the bhakti mode gave an impetus to spiritual upliftment of the commoners.

Since that time onward a synthetic and tolerant attitude to religion and social life become more prominent in that region. It is also worth mentioning that sect rivalry in any extreme form was practically not found.

2.4. Long before the Muslim invasion vaiṣṇavism took root in Bengal. Śri Jayadeva the court poet of Lakṣmana Sena composed the Gita Govinda. His dasāvatara stotra shows that Bhagavān Buddha was established as one of the avatars of Visnu in 12th century A.D. Mahāprabhu liked very much to sing and listen to Jayadeva's kāvya. He used to recite and listen to Śrimad Bhāgavatam. He used to sing songs composed by Mādhavendra Puri. Mahāprabhu liked very much to participate in dramatical performance. He derived inspiration form Śrimad Bhāgavatam. The principle of self realisation in the form of ecstatic devotion is believed to be originated form Mādhavendra Puri. The tradition of an admixturous development of the views of Śamkara and Śridhara-Svamin took a definite shape in Śri Caitanya Mahāprabhu. He had a great admiration for Śridhara Svamin's interpretation of Bhāgavatam. Śri Caitanya belonged to the dasnāmi order of Śamkara sannyasin. There is no doubt that the decadent situation in religious life, the type of scholastic system of learning and the mechanical observance of fixed duties in the Smārta system of life gave no satisfaction to the man who came back form Gaya with a new taste of devotional fervour and inward awakeing. He did not oppose the established social order or challenge the authority of any interpretation of Vedanta. He threw himself to the path of devotion and renounce the world to become a seeker of Kṛṣṇa. He did not preach a new religion.

He admitted the principles of right living following the cardinal virtues sharing the general trend of all Indian piety and morality. He recognized the institution of caste in the social matter, but in the spiritual matter he imparted a growing sense of equality and fellowship. His approach was to expound the idea of Brahmananda-rasa-satya-siva-sundara, these aspects are mentioned in Śruti. According to him the mādhurya aspect of Kṛṣṇa is predominantly manifested at Vṛndavana. One of his mission was to discover the places connected with the sacred memory of Kṛṣṇa. His disciples reclaimed such places and transformed them into places of pilgrimage. To Sri Caitanya the aspect of mādhurya rasa is the essence of God-head.[3]

2.5. The term bhakti has a special connotation-it is conceived as a subjective emotion, 'rasa'. Also the term implies loving adoration of a personal God-a simple form of worship and emotional communion. A bhakta is a devotee, his dominant feeling should be the love for the Deity. The emotional conception is a deep sentiment through which the whole personality of bhakta can be transcended. Self transcending love and devotion can lead man to the highest state of realisation. To the Vaiṣṇavas the highest state of such realisation is attributed as mahābhāta - the condition in which the self is completely absorbed. From the biographical records we find that such absorption occurred in Śri Caitanya's last phase of life very often. A kind of divine madness used to seize him of an on. The sight of the deity in the Jagannath temple, hearing music with the name of Kṛṣṇa, the sight of the blue sky, the blue ocean used to transcend his normal consciousness. Very often at night in a state of trance Śri Caitanya used to leave his room and his associates most of the time would find him in the flower garden lying unconscious. To revive his normal consciousness always they used to sing loudly the name of Kṛṣṇa. Once in such an emotional rapture he jumped into the sea. A fisherman caught him unconscious in the fishing net. Śri

Caitanya's associates searching him everywhere, informed king Prataparudra and at dawn came to the sea shore in search of him, there they found the pale body of their master. Although they thought that the end is near, they did not give up the hope and began to chant loudly the name of Kṛṣṇa. Mahāprabhu regained consciousness.

We have not heard such occurrence in other mediaeval saints lives except Śri Caitanya and Mīrābāi. The scriptural description became evident in Śri Caitanya's activities. The scriptures mention that the realised one becomes absorbed and experiences a profound joy which seems impossible to communicate in human language.

3. The works of the disciples that laid the foundation of Caitanya school of Vaiṣṇavism are :

Bhaktirasāmṛta sindhu Ujjvla nīlamani	Rupa Gosvami and Jiva Gosvami
Gopala Campu, SaṭSandarbha	Jiva Gosvami
Bhāgavata	Sanātana Gosvami
Śri Śri Hari bhakti vilāsa	Gopala Bhaṭṭa
Śri Śri Govinda līlāmṛta	Krsnadāsa Kavirāja
Govinda bhāṣya	Baladeva Vidyābhusana

These works are considered as authoritative by the Caitanya vaiṣṇava school. It is believed that Iśvara Puri transmitted the Rādha Kṛṣṇa cult to Śri Caitanya and he took the detail idea form Rāya Rāmananda. The bhakti or the loving adoration is described as a steady devotion for the personal deity, believing that the deity is the highest spiritual Being with whom a devotee can conceive an association. This mental attitude is considered to be the most important constituent of bhakti. Also the name and the deity are considered to be indentical, *i.e.*, the name and its reference can not be differentiated - nām nāni abhinna. To

Caitanya followers Kṛṣṇa is the infinite all pervanding eternal Brahman in human form, ānanda is the substance, sat and cit are His attributes. All other deities and their names attributes which appear in religious scriptures and texts are but His different manifestations.

3.1. The world process is Kṛṣṇa's līlā. The Vṛndāvana is the celestial region where the eternal līlā is going on (of His rasa aspect). He enjoys it through His own power of activity. Śri Rādha is His creation form His hlādini śakti. Kṛṣṇadāsa Kaviraja says due to His own strong desire He came down form relishing the sweetness and beauty of love for Him, also to make His devotees to relish His sweetness. After a few centuries another Bengali poet expressed the similar idea in a composition.

Jiva Gosvami explains the relation between the Jiva and Brahman as one of 'acintya bhedāveda' which maintains that God is one with and different form His creation. When the duality and non-duality is grasped or experienced that state is the state of vijñāna. In that state phenomental world man God all become one. This is abheda in realisation. The veda is from the point of view of relational knowledge. However, the relation is inexplicable because of the nature of its simultaneous difference and non-difference.

3.2. An all round perfection of personality through religious practices is the aim of vaiṣṇavism. Through religious practices our outgoing urges can be directed inwardly, to realise our true self and the goal of human life. Vaiṣṇavism gives emphasis on the emotional and volitional approach. It recommends to cultivate an attitude of surrender to the Lord. The process of surrendering is described in the nine principles of Bhagavata. The accessories are worship, study, showing respect, devoted service, keeping company of holy men, following ethical injuctions, contemplating Vṛndavana līlā, and chanting the holy name. The essential qualities a devotee should have – humility, tolerance, respectfulness, honesty, simplicity, sincerity, and contentment. To cultivate and develop these a devotee must refrain from jealously, self indulgence and self aggrandizement. With these practices a gradual and steady growth is assured, and by the grace of God a devotee may become completely free from worldly concern, his mental attitude could be transformed. At that stage the devotee may feel a strong attachment to Kṛṣṇa, this is the stage of divine love, *i.e.*, Kṛṣṇa rati; it can develop to such an extent that the devotee feels that Kṛṣṇa belongs to him or her only - and at that state of mind his behaviour may appear like a mad man - loughing, crying, dancing or be rapturous in joy. Such ecstatic expressions of spiritual experience are vividly described by kṛṣnadāsa kaviraja in his Caitanya Caritāmṛta. He has explained that Lord Kṛṣṇa incarnated Himself to enjoy the purified emotion, love and sentiments of His devotees. This is the primary reason of His being manifested in human form.

The type of salvation Caitanya followers long for is - prāpti, the loving dedicated service to Śri Kṛṣṇa. Śri Caitanya expressed in his Śikṣāṣṭaka that other type of salvation is not endering to him, he longed for 'ahaituki bhakti' - unqualified, spontaneous devotion to the Lord in this life and after - 'mama janmani janmani'. This establishes that life is not a bondage to the vaiṣṇavas, nor do they desire mukti or nirvana in the sense of cessation of birth.

4. A body of vast literature was produced by the vaiṣṇavas both in Bengali and in Sanskrit. The literary activities of the vaiṣṇavas can be accounted in its two

successive phases - the one which consists of the works of such men who were inspired by the master himself, and the other which consists of the works of the later followers. These include both works produced by the followers of Śri Caitanya at Navadvipa and Vṛndavana. I have already mentioned the authoritative treatises. Among several biographies Caitanya Caritamṛta is most favourite to the Caitanya vaiṣṇava. The contemporary Socio-political life is very well portrayed in other biographics.

4.1. The most remarkable development in post Caitanya religious thought in Bengal is a synthetic outlook; simplified mental adoration and belief in revelation of truth through emotional fervour are also prominent. The devotional attitude the divine grace are believed to be capable of nullifying the karma. The highest mood is considered to be the mystical ecstasy - to be immersed in the blissful joy when the self feels oneness with the Absolute. There is no aim, no desire to fulfil any shortcoming. Kṛṣṇa is the essential form and Rādha is the symbol of jiva, the creation of His hlādini sakti. The divine activity - the world activity is spontaneous, unconditional, aimless - a graceful enjoyment; it is nothing but His own display in His self delight. The ideal is the eternal Vṛndāvana līlā where life is a harmonious celebration in beauty, melody duty and joy. The essence of the divine is here, surrendering the ego man can realise the eternal relation of man and God; this life is not to be escaped but to live in a creative world in establishing that relation ship. Life is not a bondage.

These themes are expressed in fascinating charm in Bengali literature and music. Medieval Bengali literature was flourished by the creation of the vaiṣṇavas. They produced vast literature of devotional songs, philosophical treatises, stories, biographical works, dramatical writings, stotros, and kavyas. The alluring themes, imagery analogy are still in use in Bengali literature, music and dance. The vaiṣṇava festivals are very much alive and are enjoyable aspects of social life in the region.

4.2. Vaiṣṇavism recommends that individuals should choose the desired relationship according to individual's taste, temperament and capacity. The position of householder is no bar to follow the spiritual discipline. Most propagators of Caitanya-vaiṣṇavism in Bengal are householders. Śri Caitanya himself advised abadhuta sannyasi Nityananda to become a householder and take the leadership. There are four classes among the vaiṣṇavas in Bengal :

(*a*) Gosvamis, the gurus of the sect

(*b*) Grihasthas, the householders

(*c*) Vairagis, the ascetics

(*d*) Jat Vairagis, the 'householders having no caste standing'.

Caitanya followers who settled in Vṛndāvana are all ascetic Gosvamis. Sri Jiva Gosvami formed an Association in sixteenth century with the name 'Sri viśva Vaiṣṇava Raja Sabhā' for the propagation of Caitanya Vaiṣṇavism. It was revived by Śrila Thakur Bhaktivinode in 1886, which is known as Gauḍiya Mission. The Mission has established several centres in India and abroad. In 1965 the International Society for Kṛṣṇa Consciousness was founded by A.C. Bhaktivedanta Swami. This Society has many centres in different countries. The founder ācārya A.C. Bhaktivedanta Swami is the third in disciple succession of Srila Thakur Bhaktivinode who was the pioneer of the Gouḍiya Mission. The term 'Kṛṣṇa Consciousness' is a literal translation of the master's name 'Kṛṣṇa Caitanya'.

Last Words

In conclusion it may be said that the eastern region of India which was never a stronghold of the Vedic religion in its ancient from, except in the higher stratum, there grew in the society at large a sort of dissatisfaction due to the rigid caste system and sectarianism, also grew a sort of condemnation of the orthodox practice during the late medieval period. Due to the Muslim conquest the higher stratum of the society became shaky. In such a state of political uncertainly and social dissatisfaction in general, people found a kind of mental satisfaction in Śri Caitanya's spiritual message, and the simple process of chanting the holy name, congregation, joining in the procession rouse a sense of togetherness and security. People derived a kind of psychological support form these activities, and they readily accepted Caitanya vaiṣṇavism. Poets and preachers sang the glory of the Lord and spread the teachings of the master throughout the length and breadth of the country, and brought a change in the religious social and cultural life of the society.

Perhaps in the recent times a similar sort of displeasure has driven many young Westerners to look for a change, and some of them must have found peace pleasure and satisfaction in joining the International Society for Kṛṣṇa Consciousness.

NOTES AND REFERENCES

1. These verses are quoted in Dilip Kumar Mukherjee's book, p. 6-7.
2. These verses are quoted in Viman Behari Mojumder's book, p. 523.
3. Om satyam jnanamanantam ananda rupam amrtam
   yadvibhakti santam sivam advaitam.

Upanisad

Can be compared with,

brahmānandam parama sukhadam kevalam jnanamurtim
dvandātitam gagana sadrisam tatvamasyādilakshyam
ekam nityam vimalam acalam sarvādhisākṣhibhutam
bhābātitam triguna rahitam sadgurum tam namami.

Guru Vandana

All translations of the verses are done by the author, except the verse No. 3.

4. Ravindranath Tagore, tāi tomār ānanda...

REFERENCES

De, S.K. The Early History of the Vaisnava Faith and Movement in Bengal 1961, Firma K.L. Mukhopadhyay, Calcutta.

Mojumder, Viman Behari, Caitanya Cariter Upadan, 1955, Calcutta University.

Mojumder, A.K., Caitanya : His Life and Doctrine, 1969 Bharatiya Vidya Bhavan, Bombay.

Mukherjee, Dilip Kumar, Caitanya, 1970, National Book Trust, India, New Delhi.

Roy, Benoy Gopal, Religious Movements in Modern Bengal, 1965, Visva Bharati Research Publications, Santiniketan.

The Cultural Heritage of India Vol. IV, 1969 edition, Ramakrishana Mission Institute of Culture, Calcutta.

Caitanya Caritamṛta, Kṛṣṇadasa Kavirāj Caitanya Bhagavata, Vṛndāvan dās.

THE ESSENCE OF TAGORE'S PUJA SONGS

Rabindranath Tagore was a versatile genius. He was not only a great poet, he composed songs, he was a novelist, philosopher and critic, who wrote about religion, education and society, and is revered as one of the great thinkers of modern India.

In this paper (article) I intend to address the religious aspect of his musical oeuvre with particular emphasis on the section called 'Puja'. His Puja songs, of which there are more then 600 in number, are contained in 'Gitabitan'.

In a discussion on songs, the form and melody should have been given due consideration. Although the subtle abstract ideas, emotions and sentiments are expressed through the medium of words, the total effect of music can not be gained without the sound and rhythm. For full enjoyment of Tagore's songs, both the meanings of the words and the tunes are to be appreciated. This brief discussion is limited to the exploration of 'essence' only; it deals mainly with the idea. Neither the elaborate word to word meaning nor the tune and melody will be covered.

The aim of this paper is to pinpoint the fundamental current of unity in thought that has continued through out the centuries in India with reference to the work of Tagore.

1. Tagore was one of the most self-absorbed and emotional writers. His songs are deeply influenced by his religious philosophy, which is undogmatic and romantic.

The essence of both Vedanta and Vaisnava philosophy found beautiful expression in Tagore's musical creation. It is a superb combination of emotional sentiment and sublime spiritual feeling.

The intimate relationship between god, man and nature is the core of Tagore's philosophy. The Puja songs are mainly prayer and adoration. But this prayer is not just a formal plea for worldly prosperity; his prayers are for the upliftment of the human mind, and his songs of adoration contain no identification of any Hindu deity. Tagore glorifies the Infinitude of inexhaustible multiplicity.

The major themes of these songs are :

(*i*) appreciation of the beauty and splendour of nature as the manifestation of the Infinite, and

(*ii*) the impressive expression of the absolute all pervasive Spirit as the source and support of the world appearance.

Historically, many Puja songs can be categorized in the following manner :

1. adoration offered to light,
2. sublimation of the human spirit,
3. praise of harmony,
4. glorification of truth and explication of the Infinite as truth, beauty, bliss and eternal light,
5. glorification of the benevolent nature of the Infinite,
6. submission of ego-consciousness,
7. humanization of the Infinite and establishment of an intimate relationship,
8. the pangs of separation,

9. the journey of the soul,
10. aspiration for freedom from limitation/the quest for the beyond,
11. sensing the touch of divinity in temporal life,
12. imagining a romantic (love) relationship with God (love offering of a devotee).

These same themes can be traced form the Upaniṣads, through the Dhammapada, the Bhagavadgita, the mediaeval bhakti cult and the later Vaisnava-baul movement to the modern day work of Tagore, though there are differences in language, viewpoints and styles, reflecting the different stages of social development.

2. Avoiding the arguments and controversial aspects of different viewpoints, we can comment that in theme and imagery Tagore is a dvaitavadi, although in many of his philosophical discourses he is a thorough going advaita Vedantist. In his songs, saguna Brahman the Sovereing Lord, was his inspiration; the path of love and loving surrender to the Infinite is the main philosophical content.

Tagore sings :

No, I will never shut the doors or my senses,
The delights of sight and hearing and touch will bear Thy delight.

(*Gitanjali*)

The concept of dualism is predominent in his musical compositions. The idea of bliss which is so prominent in Upanisads and which sustains the Vaisnava Lilavad is one of the sources for Puja songs.

The poet sings :

How far is the abode of bliss.

(aro kato dure ache se anandadham)

(*Gitanjali*)

Tagore blended his appreciation of nature and beauty with devotion. This combination of nature, beauty and devotion with God consciousness has given rise to the unique emotional and spiritual fervour of his songs.

The feeling of harmony behind the pluralistic structure is the central theme; the combination of poetic expression and sublime melody exerts a transcendental effect on the mind.

Experience cannot be transmitted but it can be described. The outpourings of the Seers illumine others, and poetic compositions do likewise. Spiritual enlightenment is personal and subjective so too is the delight gained form music.

Tagore's Vaisnava faith is characterised as 'the divinizing of man and humanizing of God'.

He sings :

(*i*) you sing through my love
(amar preme tomar vani meshe)

(*ii*) O Thou Lord of all heavens, where would be thy love if I were not?
(amae noile tribhuvaneswar tomar prem hoto je miche)

(*iii*) He it is, the innermost one, who awakens my being with His deep hidden touches. (ke go antarataro se)

(*Gitanjali*)

As a bhakta he wants to surrender his ego-consciousness :

Hold done my head to your feet
(āmār māthā nato kore dāo he tomār carano dhulār tale)

He emphasises the finite - infinite nature of finite man because God Himself desires a loving relationship with the bhakta.

The experience of pleasure and pain in the course of human life gives rise to the realisation :

I did not realise that you came to my side when I was in distress.
(je rate mor duārguli bhānglo jhoṛe jāni nāito tumi ele amar ghore)

Tagore sings the gospel of love, beauty, compassion, bliss and peace. He has loved this earth with its variety of colour and sound. And his interpretation of human nature is based soundly on its cosmic and divine implications.

To him liberation lies not in the soul's absorption in Brahman; he prefers to feel God's presence in all the innumerable kinds of relationship that occur in the course of life. He aspires to realise mukti here in this world through colour, sound, touch and relationship.

Deliverance lies not for me in renunciation. I feel the embrace of freedom in a thousand bonds of delight.
(vairāgya sādhane mukti se āmār noy, asankhya bandhan mājhe labhiva muktir swād)

In Tagore's own wards : '...it (realisation?) has followed the current of my temperament from early days until it suddenly flashed into my consciousness with a direct vision'. He stated that music is the best means of knowing the Supreme Reality, because it is based on feeling. He conceived the benevolent form of the Lord of this Universe.

Satya mangala premamaya tumi
dhruvajyoti tumi andhakāre/

Truth, auspiciousness and love is His true form, compassion is His nature, and the Lord is the eternal light.

To Tagore the truth is not separate form man or his environment. He asserts that man is the best creation because:

O Lord, to all things you give;
from me you ask.

He admits that realisation comes as a gradual process of development in the human mind. Man's spirituality arises form his own heart; ethics can not be won form knowledge of the universe. The inward experience leads to the outward moral life, and that enables man to realise the peaceful co-existence of life in nature and the enduring order.

Tagore's view is that religion is a quest for greater self; it is an awareness of the (Universal Spirit) beyond.

apnake ei jānā āmār phurābenā/
ei jānāri sange sange tomay jānā//

There is no end of knowing myself and through this endeavour of knowing my innerself I will come to know You.

Through ethical practice, feeling and intuition man can encounter something beyond the senses. Though human existence is not a state of unmixed joy, this life is important because it gives the opportunity to search for truth and to realise the Infinite. Ethical excellence leads to the elavation of character. The divine is present here in the finite world; thus this temporal order is not separate form the timeless eternity.

These ideas are expressed in beautiful imagery and sublime motifs through an extraordinary variety of moods and in unparallel language.

Throughout his writings he refers to the deity of his life as 'jivan devata', which the critics identify with the poet's personal deity. The Universal Spirit, whom Tagore addressed as 'Visva devata'. His feeling of universalism is expressed as 'satya sei cirantan ak' "the Truth is one" :

> **The same stream of life that runs**
> **through my veins night and day runs through**
> **the world and dances in rhythmic measures.**
>
> (*Gitanjali*)

Footnotes

1. Gitanjali (*Song offerings*) by Rabindranath Tagore, Macmillion and Co. Limited, London. 1928 edition.
2. Gitabitan, Rabindranath Tagore, Visvabharati, 1958 edition.

THE RESOLUTION OF INNER CONFLICT

The aim of this short paper is to point out the fundamental values (following the Gita) which ought to be maintained in human life for progress.

One way to deal with our problems is to develop our awareness of reality. Reality in the sense of reciprocal relationship between individual man and the immediate society in the perspective of world society. This awareness can be developed through the study of religious philosophy.

Such awareness could help a person to advance one's total human development. At one time or other an intelligent person might enquire of oneself - what do I live for ? If one finds some answers, probably a balanced and unprejudiced personality would develop, which can mould one's attitude to life and can restrict reactions in many unfavourable situations in life. The right attitude to life and a balanced personality held by the majority has a great bearing on the society.

1. Religion is part of life there is no doubt about it. Some may not agree with me but many will. I strive to find out the way and means to relate the teachings meaningfully to my life. So neither metaphysical inquiry nor eschatological or seteriological speculation fascinate me. I am conditioned with Hindu ideas. I cannot boast that I have conceived the ideas fully. As far as I have understood that the three aspects of religion laymen involved in are; understanding the

fundamentals, the methods which assure measured benefit, and following tradition.

Mostly, laymen accept the authority and expect authoritative guidance. May be this submission makes one incapable of viewing his society and social values critically.

They see the teachings and guidance do have reflection on life, they observe. When the interplay of contradictory and conflicting socio-political and economic forces strongly react on common-man's life, it results in possible confusion of basic human values.

With the advancement of science and technology and the availability of technological facilities man's egoism has strengthened. The sceptic intellectualism and biased secularism have brought much more bewilderment. We are no more in peace, we have lost our satisfaction, we are not contented.

From childhood to the old age mostly we spend in tention and restless pursuit for aimless goal. We struggle for survival not with nature but with economic disparity, international threat and moral degradation. In this traumatic situation it is futile to seek God. Perhaps in the end realisation comes that much time and energy have been wasted in worthless pursuit of competition to satisfy our greed and to console our ego.

The modern tactics cum strategy to tackle this aggravated situation is either by forcing economic repression or by instigating endless temptation and competition for capturing economic hierarchy. Enormous possession of wealth is the highest goal in life.

On the contrary, the ancient society showed the prospect of a more just and human world to live in by advocating 'dharma', by moulding life in a different way. Visualising the ultimate destiny of human life, more emphasis was given to the attainment of peace of mind. Neither any clearcut compartmentalism in life was emphasised nor the sharp line of distinction was drawn between the virtues of social conduct and spiritual. The relative importance of the basic human necessities for preservation and smooth maintenance of life was there but sole importance to material life only was not the aim. The extreme emphasis on economic achievement and material wealth is one of the main malady of modern mind. Again the idea that man's particular urges and drives need not be checked. This may be the central point that by satisfying only the instinctive priorities man cannot claim to be the rational one, man must cultivate a higher taste of spiritual life, because every living entity possesses the spark of energy which emanates form the universal source of energy. This acceptance of universal source stresses the divinity and unity in human beings. Hence there arises the necessity to mould human life towards the unfolding of inner divinity and strive for self realisation.

2. No other ideologies of isms except spiritualism can provide proper understanding of the position of an individual in the context of human race and eternal time. It is also doubtful if other isms can ever provide any incentive for achievement of a blissful state of mind.

Sanatana dharma, 'an eternal religion', which is widely termed as Hindu religion encompasses an wide range of thoughts. The most profound is that the realisation of Brahman within the self and then in outer reality, is not just abstract reasoning, it can't be fully explained in human language, it is beyond reason and logical speculation of mind. That highest state of mind, is termed as 'turiya abastha' in Indian philosophy. It can be experienced by any one who strives his utmost to free himself form the scum and rust of worldliness. This ultimate consciousness is regarded as the suprasensuous experience. Although it happens in the existence of the physical body and through the sense instrument of mind, it is beyond the ordinary sense level and the level of intellect. This extraordinary quality is attributed as 'cidsakti'. Without penetrating to the philosophical question of the difference between mind and matter and the possible existence of such suprasensuous level of mind, I would simply remark that accepting this quality and capacity of human mind Hindu philosophy views human potency form a very different angle. Hindus firmly believe that truths revealed in that state of mind are recorded in scriptures. And in no way we can neglect what is instructed in scriptures for the common men to observe in every day life, there by to prepare themselves for higher understanding. Even though the transcendental experience can only be attained by the perfect living personalities, it is open to all. As soul is eternal and individual's soul journeys through the cycle of birth and death, merits can gradually be accumulated. Therefore this station of life is not meant to be wasted in self-indulgence and sense-gratification, rather by application of intelligence the message of the teaching has to be understood, by practising recommended instruction self discipline has to be achieved and through rightful activities obligations, duties have to be discharged. By doing so in every day life a right attitude to life can be developed and this is essential for every social human being for peace, tranquility in mind, happiness in life and harmonious living in the society. That is considered to be the ideal situation in collective life and the ideal condition in individual's mind to develop consciousness. That is the favourable condition for correct understanding of the existing position of individual and the purpose of human life.

3. I would concentrate on the Bhagavad Gita and would try to put forward the subjective implication of its teaching. The Gita is a harmonious blending of 'sruti' and other disciplines. The teaching of Gita is for practical living and for spiritual guidance.

It proclaims the transitoriness of this life, ephemeral nature of all material objects and the soul's eternity (na hanayāte hanyamāne sharīre).

It stresses that due to the mode of material nature worldly life is bound to be sorrowful. Through the natural process inevitably there occurs change, growth, decay and death to the gross body. Fitting to this natural process the significant pattern of 'caturāsharm' has been evolved. As a matter of fact no living entity can escape this process.

Also there is self evident inborn inequality in man. There are differences in intellectual capacity, ability, physical strength, temperament, quality, psychological tendency etc. The Gita explains that basically, three modes of nature dominate in human beings : some are prone to evil, some are good, some are influenced and easily distracted by passion and impulses. Every individual has in him or her these three modes, sometimes one predominates the other. Therefore every one needs to try to control his mind. Uncontrolled and unstable mind can not hold any good firmly. Both subjectively and objectively to achieve a good and harmonious living individual members of the society has to make a balance in mental and physical growth. The one is complementary to the other. Subjectively mental maturity is beneficial for healthy and peaceful living.

The material prosperity needs to be balanced with responsibility and obligation. Man has rationality so he possesses the awareness of self; he should control his behaviour in all human relationship. It is not enough for him or her to be true to his or her natural condition.

3.1. The four stages of life (caturāsharma) are : the period of mental cultivation through education and the stage of physical culture; the second stage is the household, when normal persons require to satisfy their emotional urges, there is need for marriage and family life, accepting social obligation and family responsibilities a healthy household to be maintained; in the third stage physical needs gradually reduce, maturity grows, one has to withdraw oneself gradually form attachment; in the fourth stage on longer social services are required from the individual.

Right form the beginning, through the formative age one should be taught the purpose of the self disciplinary principles, the purpose of human life; at the mature age individual should take up the path of dharma and lead a good life and gradually try to elevate the mind. The key conception of the term dharma includes :

(*i*) the inheritance of merit form the previous birth, which is called 'purva-sanskāra';

(*ii*) the acquisition of the family duty, obligated occupation ('swadharma');

(*iii*) the obligatory maintenance of the universal code.

These concept constitute the meaning of the term dharma, the root means that which supports. Although man has legitimate desires for 'artha' or wealth, material prosperity and 'kama' or sense pleasure because instinctive necessitive have to be fulfilled. But 'artha' and 'kāma' should never supersede 'dharma' and 'moksha'. No matter what position one holds in the society or in the family, what caste or stratum of the society (vaṛnā) he/she belongs to or which stage of life he/she is in, one should practise discipline for self control and cultivate mental faculty. By surrendering one's ego and selfish motive one can elevate the mind. The dichotomy of 'caturāshrama' and 'verṇāshrama' is natural and ideal, they are not contradictory forces but an acceptable gradation and a fitting pattern of life situation in human society.

Although the goal of life is the same for all men, truths are universal, the requirements for higher attainment are same, till differences have to be accepted. There is neither such thing as universal ṣtandard of duty, nor all men could rationally be expected to comprehend the same concept. But every normal social human being has a function : the prime function is to become rational : through the path of dharma, raising the mind towards a higher morality, one needs to develop a right attitude to life. The Gita insists that the way of conflict and conquest in the physical sense is not the proper way.

Since technology, science and secular education assert man's ego the way of conflict and conquest seems to be the only way we can think of in modern terms. There is no doubt that modern education leaves open an enquiring mind, but that mind is going to be tearing apart if it does not enter into the deep enquiry of any subject matter. The vastness of the world, the vastness of human knowledge and the relative insignificance of an individual can not be conceived at the lower level of inquiry. So it insists and encourages to establish man's ego. And most of our problems in personal life and in social life are ego centric.

Paradoxically, the Gita stresses that man needs to surrender his ego. This is very significant. The submission and dedication are the prior necessities to achieve any goal. For deep enquiry, to get the insight we need perseverance, patience faith and submission. Unless we can give up our egotism we can not get rid of our selfish desires, our pride of designation, arrogance, greed, excessive emphasis on self. And we all know that due to this exclusive self importance there arise constant conflict - clash with other in every phases of life. Sometimes it is demonstrated in violent actions in personal life, social life, and in international situation, which aggravate harmonious co-existence, peaceful living. On the contrary, if one can control his mind, check his egotistic mentality and feel obligated to discharge his duties and responsibilities without being carried away by impulses, then his behaviour in all kinds of relationship will certainly improve. This would surely be reflected in collective life. If one understands his limitation in respect of ability, intellect, available opportunity etc. he may not feel frustrated if he can not achieve higher material prosperity. Again, egotistic mentality develops a kind of biasness, due to that often the tendency to disrespect, non-appreciation, underestimation come, envy and jealousy grow up. If one can surrender one's ego then, on the one hand these tendencies would gradually wither away; on the other hand even in underestimation, indignity and injustice one can forgive the other who caused these. Neither one will feel too depressed nor he will think of taking revenge. Also self submission would highly engender the feeling of appreciation.

However, it does not rule out that such individual or community would not be disadvantaged or exploited. But as I mentioned before that Hindu philosophy and ethics focussed the good and there is an expectation man would be able to transform his character through the rightful activities in life.

3.2. One has to develop an attitude that whatever comes in the course of life has to be accepted with ease. Since the expected span of human life does not permit one to develop many talents; according to one's capacity, intelligence, temperament and opportunity whichever jobs and tasks one gets to accomplish one should do with ease considering the job, the task as allocated to him; also what ever situation arises one has to accept it calmly because there is no choice. We can not choose our parents, we can not choose our birth place, many other things on which we have no control. This attitude of acceptance would develop a sense of eqanimity. This will avart frustration.

These understanding seem to be the essence of the teaching for practical living. Also these seem to be the psychological basis of self discipline and mental control, which can resolve many of our conflict-confusion, suffering and anxieties. Our feeling of hatred, prejudice, envy, desire for sense pleasure, sex appetite, vanity, temptation, anger, aggressive tendency, power hankering, greed for money and possession cause mental ill. We loose our energy in restless distraction caused by these tendencies. We need to reverse the process by a gradual re-adjustment of outlook and habit-formation.

There is no doubt that we pray for blessing, we pray for mercy, benediction we wish that good things would bestow upon us. But if we could surrender ourselves, probably we would have been saved form much of our mental sufferings.

4. The Bhagavad Gita expounds that if one follows the recommended discipline offensive mental waves will be controlled and his attitude is bound to change. According to individual's intelligence, ability and temperament four different paths are advocated, several steps of self discipline

are instructed and for the householders obligated duties are advised.

It is said that for thoughtful persons there are choices:

One can control the mind and develop 26 qualities such as, strightforwardness, simplicity, modesty, tolerance, compassion, non-anger, non-aggression, non-temptation, non-injury, non-egotistic attitude, calmness etc. by means of observing austerity and other discipline. By practising gradual steps in every day life together with the gradual withdrawal form material-emotional attachment one can develop a balanced personality a transformed character.

All Hindu scriptures, yogies, saints, gurus proclaimed that the secret of life is neither in sense gratification nor in highest possession of material wealth but education through life's experience - the goal is an awareness of the individual's position in the context of human race and eternal time, this awareness causes an awakening within the self, which is above any kind of sentimentalism. It is not a creed, not a dogma, not any kind of institutionalism, not any sectarian outlook. This awareness is the key conception to the progress of humanity, and the remedy to the malady of conflict and clash. When that awakening comes, it becomes easier to achieve the blissful state of mind.

4.1 There are structured instructions for all :

Yama : The ethical principles, the basic rules of conduct to be maintained by all, the high and the low. The austerity to be maintained bodily mentally and verbally.

(*i*) Reverence for devas, the seers, the teachers, the sages, the parents, straightforwardness, harmlessness, physical cleanliness and sexual purity these are bodily austerity.

(*ii*) Saying what is beneficial to other, causing no pains to other by words, reading scriptures, chanting holy names-verbal austerity can be maintained.

(*iii*) Purifying the motive by higher thinking, feeling sympathy and compassion to other, silent repetition of mantra - mental austerity to be maintained.

The positive aspect of these principles are to become good, honest in words thoughts and actions. Particularly, non-injury - the abstention form harming others is extremely significant, if one can truly develop that understanding then the tendency of crime, killing, violent expression and action can be checked. Also greed, disrespect, ill feeling, animosity, resentment will gradually diminish.

Secondly one has to practise 'niyama' - the religious discipline by acquiring regular habit of study and worship. Rituals are also important to create an environment.

Thirdly, several 'āsanas' - postures are recommended for attaining concentration and good health. Since the mind and body are closely related, emotions cause change in the body and changes in the body arouse emotions in the mind. When one sits in a position, mental waves come and gradually settle down, in that state of mind self analysis can be possible. Many of our wrong actions, wrong choices and indecisions can be rectified by self analysis. The inner poise depends mostly on the adjustability and acceptability of various events, ups and downs in the course of life.

For the householder the habit of charity is instructed. Common men are not neutral personalities like śanyasis (monks), they are involved in social life. Those are lucky who possess material wealth, that has to be shared with others. Actually, nothing belongs to any body, every thing is allocated, we should do the work and get the reward and remuneration for self preservation and healthy family life, there is no need for excess. The Gita lay stress on charity and on the moderation of eating, drinking, sleeping, sex and recreation habit.

The fourth step is 'prānāyāma' - with 'āsana', 'prānāyāma' to be practised, 'prānāyama' is the breathing control which results calmness in mind. Practice of 'āsana' and 'prānāyāma' can reduce tentions and restlessness. Through the observance of austerities mentioned, and these self disciplinary accessories one can cultivate an equilibrium of body and mind.

The fifth, sixth and seventh steps are 'pratyāhāra', 'dharana' and 'dhayāna'. Sitting quietly, exercising breathing control in order to gain calmness of the mind, one can try to free the mind from the bewilderment of the sense, that is the step of 'pratyāhāra'. Then the step of concentration, gradual fixation of mind on a single thought, which is called 'dhārana'.

The next step is meditation-'dhyāna'. 'Samādhi' is the highest state of super consciousness. It is stressed that each step a small step is leading to the higher scale of life in awakening towards the higher moral attitude and to the ultimate goal of spiritual consciousness, the realisation of universal truth. 'vaśe hi yasyendriyāṇi tasya prajñā pratiṣṭhitā'–when one attains the balanced state of mind by controlling his senses, he become pure in heart, calm and dispassionate in spirit, the mode of goodness prevails in him, he become a man of steady intelligence. In that state one can see the truth, (ch.2,T.6I). In an unmistakable language it is mentioned that lust, rage and greed these lead to ruin of human potentialities : kāma eṣa krodha eṣa rajoguṇa-samudbhava mahāśano mahāpāpmā viddhy enam iha vairiṇam / āvṛtaṁ jñānam etena jñānino nitya vairiṇā kāmarūpeṇa kaunteya duṣpūreṇānalena ca (ch. 3, T, 37/39).

5. Precisely the four different paths of attainment expounded in Gita are 'jñāna yoga; the path of knowledge, 'raja-yoga' - the path of meditation, 'bhakti - yoga' - the path of love and devotion and 'karma-yoga' - the path of activity, selfless service to mankind.

Perhaps reconciliation of all these paths is the ideal for man. But it is not easy to blend them in one individual personality. The vital point is neither the path of knowledge nor the path of action can be thought of devoiding spiritual realisation.

Those who are emotional, those who are rational, those who are introspective and active and those who wish to contemplate abstract ideal, those who need concrete symbol for worship and ritual to follow all can get incentive for solace in 'sanātana - dharma'. The path of knowledge, the path of meditation, the path of devotion and the path of action all lead to the same - the realisation of God who is in individual self and in outer reality. Here I would like to quote a passage :

'Each of these yogas is an independent path to God, and when the end is attained, all four seem to join together in one. Supreme love, divine knowledge, true meditation, and true and divine action are at last identical and cannot be differentiated form one another. The Gita insists that they must all be practised. Man is a complex of faculties - reason, will, emotion, and the impulse to action - and he must seek union with God through all of them. He must be active as well as meditative; he must cultivate his intelligence and seek the supreme knowledge as well as cultivate love for the Divine Being - such, in short, is the yoga ideal as taught in the Gita.

Jñāna yoga literally means the path of union through knowledge. It has come to connote intellectual analysis leading to the immediate preception (anubhuti) of God, who is both transcendent and immanent, who is the inner reality of both man and the external universe. Philosophical reasoning does not imply mere natural ratiocination, but somethings more, for man's unaided intellect cannot lead him to God. There must be in addition a transformation of life and conduct, a conversion of the soul, before the knowledge of God, or the self, can be attained... For immediate realisation and understanding of The Self, jñāna yoga advocates that reasoning about God be followed by certain disciplines. First of all the philosopher must learn to discriminate between the real and the unreal... The only abiding reality - the immutable, the indestructible Reality - is that by which the whole universe is pervaded. It is the same as the Self in man. Whatever we perceive or sense or experience has both beginning and end; therefore must our faculty of discrimination lead us to hold fast to the enduring reality, the Self or God, in the midst of fleeting objects and experiences of life and death...Since we know the Self alone to be real, we should learn to realise in it the great source of happiness and renounce the desire for pleasure.... To follow the path of philosophy is also to follow the path of self-control, directing the mind towards the Reality... Following the path of knowledge and discrimination does not imply giving up the normal activities of life. What one is required to do is to regard the body as the house which one inhabits, and the mind and the senses as the instruments of living - to all of which the Lord is the witness. A person so doing acts but does not identify himself with his actions. He experiences the objective universe, but form this universe he has learned to detach himself.

Action... is not opposed to the highest wisdom. An individual who has attained the highest knowledge and the supreme peace, though he has nothing to gain by action, nor anything to lose by inaction, yet works, not however for his ordinary self but, through exercise of mind, senses, and body, for his true Self, which he has identified with the Lord of the universe. Never forgetful of his true Self, he is forever one with God; and knowing that the Self exists in all, he engages in the service of God in all mankind. Such a man, steady in wisdom, experiences intense rest in the midst of intense action.'[1]

Says the Gita that there is no existence without action, physical activity and mental activity are the nature of living entity. Avarting egocentricity man can develop selflessness. Common-man accepting duties, responsibilities, must try to rise above the mode of ignorance and passion by exercising self disciplinary activities in every day life and through the proper understanding of the spirit of the teaching. Gradually one must try to withdraw oneself form all kinds of attachment.

When an individual possesses calmness in mind, becomes free of passion automatically his desires are channelised to the realisation of Brahman, then the blissfulness and compassion for all prevail in him in the true sense.

> **'brahma-bhūtah prasannātmā na socati na kaṇkṣati/ samaha sarveṣu bhūteṣu madbhaktiṁ labhate parām'**
>
> *(Ch.18, S. 54).*

It is wrong to equate this bliss and tranquility with indolence and insensibility. Also it is wrong to think that self control means the repression and inhibition. It is a misconception that karma-yoga referring merely disinterested action, rather it refers to the dedicated dispassionate service to humanity knowing fully well that God exists in each living entity.

If one does not surrender one's ego then there remains demand, an urge for self reward, also there remains the possibility of self projection, self imposition and emphasis. Here lies the difference between karma-yoga and other ordinary welfare activities. Action to be performed in a spirit of love and non-attachment, and there should not be any expectation for self. This non-attachment is not indifference, it is rather a kind of inner poise - equanimity either in success or in failure.

6. Hindu philosophy affirms that only ethical discipline cannot transform man's character, unless the realization of fundamental oneness comes, it is hard to raise oneself above the narrow self.

Although we see ourselves in physical and social environment, a radical orientation of our attitude can be possible if we try to get the correct message of religious teachings. If we can feel the distress and the dignity of others and with our limited capacity we try to remove the tragedies of human society then perhaps the idea of peaceful and harmonious co-existence will come into reality. If we try to control our mind and sincerely develop the sense of non-injury, then perhaps we can have happiness within and out. It might happen in both ways: one might be so inspired that he can give up worldly life or one can prepare himself gradually step by step following the recommended instructions.

In conclusion I would say that in all ages great living personalities rediscover and reinterpret the concepts, they set examples through their activities and make the ideas more comprehensible and relevant to common men - that there is no better alternative for human progress than mental upliftment. With intellectual freedom, economic betterment the populace need spiritual consciousness.

The Gita advises :

'manmanā bhava mad bhakto mad-yājī mām namaskuru/ *(Ch. 9, Sloka 34)*

sarva-dharmān parityajya māmakaṁ śaraṇam vraja'

(Ch. 18, S. 65, 66).

Fix your mind upon God. Always think of Him and act for Him. Surrender to Him. Accomplishing your duties, detach yourself and take refuge to the peaceful blissful arena of spiritualism.

In fact no sectarianism can shroud the spirit of scriptures.

REFERENCE

1. The Spiritual Heritage of India, Swami Prabhavananda, with the assistance of Frederick Manchester, pp. 124–126. Vedanta Press, Hollywood, California, 1969 edition.

APPENDIX – B

THE DESCRIPTION OF SANSKRIT COURSE OFFERED AND STUDENTS' REMARKS

1. The joy and reverence with which Mrs Gangopadhya approaches Sanskrit is inspiring, and her patience is saint like...... I've wanted to learn Sanskrit for several years but have been unable to find a teacher.
2. I must say Mrs. Malaya Gangopadhyay's approach to the Sanskrit through the Hindu Scriptures is both refreshing and fascinating. Her personality, too, is a major contributing (factor) to her unique approach.

Course Title

Sanskrit for beginners.

Course Description

This course is designed for adult learners.

It provides basic features of the language, grammar, pronunciation practice, reading and word as well as sentence structures. It also gives some cultural information.

Objectives

to gain access in reading text in the target language,

to rouse interest in further study.

Approach to Teaching

Activities include reading aloud, writing, chanting texts collected form authentic sources. To facilitate pronunciation class participation in chanting is very useful. It also gives a traditional touch.

Materials

Students need to purchase a published text book. Pronunciation cassette is provided by CAE.

SANSKRIT

The values and wisdom, concepts and world view of a society are transmitted form generation to generation through language. With this perspective in mind we will explore Sanskrit the ancient language of India. This course introduces pronunciation, reading, study of vocabulary, sentence structure and script writing. Cultural aspects also discussed. Course notes provided.

SANSKRIT

Course provides an explanation of language features leading to reading and comprehension of authentic text written in Devanagari script. Introduces sound patterns, script, simple structures and vocabulary including essential Indian concepts. Activities include chanting of verses to facilitate pronunciation and reading. Materials provided, including pronunciation cassette.

SANSKRIT – 2

For those who have completed a CAE beginners' course can extend their knowledge of both culture and language through authentic and devotional literature. Materials including pronunciation tape, provided.

SANSKRIT – 3

Course for general interest and for those interested in devotional literature and philosophy. Introduces sound patterns, script, simple structures and vocabulary including essential Indian concepts. Activities include chanting of verses to facilitate pronunciation and reading of verses to facilitate pronunciation and reading of authentic texts. Materials provided, incl. pronunciation cassette.

BHĀSHĀBODHINĪ TRITIYA PĀTHA

This is the third and final book of compilation of the teaching materials provided for the Sanskrit course offered by the CAE in Melbourne. Although the primary focus was on learning the language, it was assumed that focussing on selected representative literary fragments and becoming acquainted with the relevant background information would be both interesting and valuable to mature students. The intention was to give a brief overview of some Indian religious and philosophical concepts including the idea of discipline. While the second book explored the meaning of devotion and the devotional path, mainly with reference to Viṣṇu and Kṛṣṇa, that in the present volume this devotional theme is continued through the study of selected texts relating to the mother Goddess and Lord Siva.

REFERENCES

1. Rigveda, Asiatic Society of Bengal, Edited by Dr. E. Roer, Calcutta, 1849.
2. The call of the Vedas, A.C. Bose, Bharatiya Vidya Bhavan, Mumbai, 1988.
3. Yayurveda, Tr. by Devi Chand, Delhi, 1980.
4. Eight Upanisads–Vol. 2, Tr. by Swami Gambhirananda, Advaita Ashram, Calcutta, 1989.
5. The Upanisads, Edited by Atul Chandra Sen, Sitanath Tattwabhusan and Mahesh Chandra Ghosh, Haraf Prokashani, Calcutta, 1980.
6. Brahmasutra, Tr. by Swami Vireswarananda, Advaita Ashram Calcutta 1982 Reprint.

7. Srimadbhagavadgita, Tr. and edited by Swami Jagadiswarananda and Swami Jagadananda, Udbodhan, Calcutta 1977 edition.
8. The Bhagavad Gita, R.C. Zaehner, Oxford Uuniversity Press, London, 1976 edition.
9. Vivekacudamani, Śri Śankaracarya, Tr. by Swami Madhavananda; Saundarya Lahari, Tr. by Pt. S. Subrahmanya Sastri and T.R. Srinivasa Ayyangar, The Theosophical Publishing House Adyar, Madras 1985.
10. Siva Sutra, Vasugupta.
11. Sadacarah of Adi Sankara, Commented by Sudhansu Caitanya, Central Cinmaya Mission Trust Publication 1988.
12. Purva Mimamsa in its sources by M.M. Dr. Ganganath Jha, Edition by Dr. S. Radhakrishnan, Banaras Hindu University Varanasi, 1964 edition.
13. Patanjali Yoga Sutras, Swami Prabhavananda and Chistopher Isherwood, Sri Ramakrishna Math, Mylopore, Madras 1994 edition.
14. The Yogasutra of Patanjali, Bengali Baba, Motilal Banarsidass Delhi 1982 Print.
15. Yoga Philosophy of Patanjali by Sankḫya–Yogāchārya Swami Hariharananda Aranya, Rendered into English by P.N. Mukerjee, State University of New York Press, Albany 1981 (first published by Calcutta University Press 1965).
16. Abhinava Gupta, K.C. Pandey, Chaukhamba Publica- tion, Varanasi 1963.
17. Chakras (Energy Centres of Transformation) by Harish Johari, Destiny Books, Vermont 1987.
18. Yantra, The Tantric Symbol of Cosmic Unity, by Madhu Khanna, Thames and Hudson Ltd., London 1979.
19. The Secret of the Vedas, Sri Aurobinda, Sri Aurobinda Ashram Pondichery, India, 1971.
20. Vedic Poem Tr. by Abinash Chandra Bose.

21. Gods, Sages and Kings, Vedic Secrets of Ancient Civilization by David Frawley, Motilal Banarsidass, Delhi 1993.
22. The Concept of Philosophy, The Centre of Advanced Study in Philosophy, Banaras HIndu University, Varanasi 1968.
23. The Philosophy of Sadhana, Deba Brata Sen Sharma, Published by The State University of New York Press, Albany, 1990 Reprint.
24. Siva Sidhanta Theology, Rohan A. Danuwila, Motilal Banarsi Dass, Delhi 1985.
25. An Advanced History of India by R.C. Majumdar, H.C. Raychaudhuri and Kalikinkar Dutta, Macmillan and Co. Limited London 1948.
26. Histoy of Sanskrit Literature, Prof. A. Macdonell, Oxford, London.
27. Philosophy of Hindu Sadhana, Nalinikanta Brahma, Motilal Banarsidass Delhi 1993 (Indian Edition).
28. The Foundation of Hindusim, Jadunath Sinha, Sinha Publishing House, Calcutta 1955.
29. An Introduction to Hinduism, Gavin Flood, Cambridge University Press 1996.
30. Religions of Ancient India, Lois Renou, Schocken Books, New York.
31. Sources of Indian Tradition Vol. 1, 2 General Editor W.M. Theodore De Bary, Columbia University Press, 1958.
32. The Art of India, Calambur Sivaramamurti, Harry N. Abrams Incorporated, New York, 1977.
33. Spiritual Heritage of India, Swami Prabhhvananda and Frederick Manchester, Vedanta Press, Hollywood, California Second Paper back Edition 1969.
34. The Cultural Heritage of India, Vol. I-V, The Ramakrishna Mission Institute of Culture, Calcutta, 1978 edition.
35. Hindu Symbology and other Essays, Swami Swahananda, Sri Ramakrishna Math, Mylapore, Madras 1987 edition

36. Vaisnavism Saivism and Minor Religious Systems, Ramakrishna Gopal Bhandarkar, Asia Publication Series, New Delhi, 1983.
37. A History of Indian Philosophy, Vol. 1-5, Surendranath Dasgupta Motilal Banarsidass, Delhi, 1988 Reprint.
38. Indian Philosophy, Vol. 1-2, S. Radhakrishnan, Oxford University Press, Delhi 1989 Centenary Edition.
39. Outlines of Indian Philosophy, Dr. Paul Deussen, Ess Ess Publication, Delhi 1976 (First Indian Reprint).
40. Outlines of Indian Philosophy, M. Hiriyanna, George Allen and Unwin (India) Limited, Bombay.
41. The Philosophical Tradition of India, P.T. Raju, George Allen and Unwin Limited, Bombay.
42. Philosophy of Ramanuja.
43. Philosophy of Nimbarka, Jadunath Sinha, Sinha Publishing House, Calcutta, 1972.
44. History of The Daivta School of Vedanta and Its Literatures, B.N.K. Sharma, Motilal Banarsidass, Delhi, Second Edition, 1981.
45. Indian psychology, Vol. 1-3, Jadunath Sinha, Motilal Banarsidass Delhi 1986 Reprint.
46. Aspect of Indian Psychology, Dinesh Chandra Bhattacharya Shastri, Ramakrishna Mission Ashram, Narendrapur, West Bengal, 1988.
47. Hindu Psychology, Swami Akhilananda, Harper and Brothers Publisher, New York, 1946.
48. Aspect of Indian Religious Thought, Sashi Bhusan Dasgupta, Firma Klm Private Limited, Calcutta 1977.
49. Psycho Analytic Concept of Religion, Dr. S.M. Tripathi, Ajanta Publication, Delhi, 1979.
50. The Structure of Indian thought, Ramakant A. Sinari, Oxford

51. Yoga as Philosophy and Religion, Surendranath Dasgupta, Motilal Banarsidass, Delhi Reprint 1978.
52. Yogo Philosophy, S.N. Dasgupta, Motilal Banarsidass. Delhi, 1979 Reprint.
53. History of the Tantric Religion, N.N. Bhattacharya, Manohar Publication, New Delhi 1982.
54. Studies on the Tantras, The Ramakrishna Mission Institute of Culture, Calcutta 1989.
55. Tantra Tattatwa Pravesika, Swami Prajnananda.
56. Tantre Tattatwa O Sadhana, Swami Prajnananda, Sri Ramakrishna Vedanta Math, Calcutta 1988.

Journals

Desh 9th November 1985, Calcutta (Ma Kali by Janhavi Kumar Chakravorty) Desh 26th October 1985, Calcutta (Chaitanyavadan by Sukumar Sen).

Desh 16th April 1988, Calcutta (Hindur Dharma by Sivjiban Bhattacharya, Anantalal Thakur, Bimalkriskna Matilal, Bimal Kar, Hitesh Ranjan Sanyal, Arindam Chakravorty, Jaynarayan Sen and Muhammad Tahir).

Nibodhata, Sri Sarada Math, Dakshineswar, Calcutta 2001, Patanjali Yoga by Govindagopal Mukhopadhyay.